INDIANA

SCIENCE

FUSIOn

fusion [FYOO • zhuhn] a mixture or blend
formed by fusing two or more things

This Interactive Student Edition belongs to

Zelda

Teacher/Room

Mis. Fish

HOUGHTON MIFFLIN HARCOURT

HOUGHTON MIFFLIN HARCOURT

Front Cover: *sea turtle* ©Westend6l GmbH/Alamy; *water bubbles* ©Andrew Holt/Alamy; *guitar and saxophone* ©Brand Z/Alamy; *giraffe* ©The Africa Image Library/Alamy; *observatory* ©Robert Llewellyn/Workbook Stock/Getty Images; *wind turbines* ©Comstock/Getty Images.

Back Cover: *ferns* ©Mauro Fermariello/Photo Researchers, Inc.; *galaxy* ©Stocktrek/Corbis; *clownfish* ©Georgette Douwma/Photographer's Choice/Getty Images; *prism* ©Larry Lilac/Alamy.

Printed in the U.S.A.

ISBN 978-0-547-43841-2

3 4 5 6 7 8 9 10 0877 19 18 17 16 15 14 13 12 11
4500300588 BCDEFG

Consulting Authors

Michael A. DiSpezio
Global Educator
North Falmouth, Massachusetts

Marjorie Frank
*Science Writer and Content-Area Reading
   Specialist*
Brooklyn, New York

Michael Heithaus
*Director, School of Environment and Society
Associate Professor, Department of Biological
   Sciences*
Florida International University
North Miami, Florida

Donna Ogle
Professor of Reading and Language
National-Louis University
Chicago, Illinois

Program Advisors

Paul D. Asimow
*Professor of Geology and
   Geochemistry*
California Institute of Technology
Pasadena, California

Bobby Jeanpierre
*Associate Professor of Science
   Education*
University of Central Florida
Orlando, Florida

Gerald H. Krockover
*Professor of Earth and Atmospheric
   Science Education*
Purdue University
West Lafayette, Indiana

Rose Pringle
*Associate Professor
   School of Teaching and Learning*
College of Education
University of Florida
Gainesville, Florida

Carolyn Staudt
Curriculum Designer for Technology
KidSolve, Inc.
The Concord Consortium
Concord, Massachusetts

Larry Stookey
Science Department
Antigo High School
Antigo, Wisconsin

Carol J. Valenta
*Senior Vice President and Associate
   Director of the Museum*
Saint Louis Science Center
St. Louis, Missouri

Barry A. Van Deman
President and CEO
Museum of Life and Science
Durham, North Carolina

Power up with Science Fusion!

Your program fuses. . .

Online Virtual Experiences

Hands-on Explorations

Active Reading

. . .to generate science energy for you.

Active Reading

Be an active reader and make this book your own!

Write your ideas, answer questions, make notes, and record activity results right on these pages.

Your book will become a record of everything you learn in science.

v

Hands-on Explorations

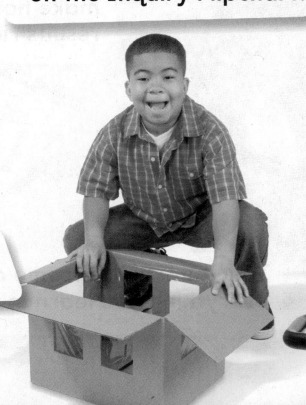

Science is all about doing.

How Does the Sun Warm Our Homes?

How does solar energy warm our homes? Make a model to find out.

Materials

cardboard box	tape
scissors	2 thermometers
plastic wrap	

① Use the box and the plastic wrap to make a model house. Caution! Be careful when using scissors.

② Tape one thermometer into a window of the house. Record the temperatures on both thermometers.

③ Put the house in a sunny spot. Lay the other thermometer next to the house. Wait 1 hour. Record both temperatures again. Compare the numbers.

Do the exciting activities on the Inquiry Flipchart.

Ask questions and test your ideas.

Draw conclusions and share what you learn.

Online Virtual Experiences

Use a computer to make science come alive.

Explore cool labs and activities in the virtual world.

Science Fusion
is new energy just for YOU!

Contents

STANDARD 1
Physical Science

© Houghton Mifflin Harcourt Publishing Company

Unit 4—Weather and the Sky 137

The Practice of Science

Lab at Purdue University,
West Lafayette, Indiana

I Wonder Why

Scientists use tools to find out about things. Why?
Turn the page to find out.

Here's Why Tools help scientists learn more than they could with only their senses.

Track Your Progress

Essential Questions and Indiana Standards

PROCESS STANDARDS
Nature of Science

Students gain scientific knowledge by observing the natural and constructed world, performing and evaluating investigations and communicating their findings. These principles should guide student work and be integrated into the curriculum along with the content standards on a daily basis.

The **Nature of Science** Students gain scientific knowledge by observing the natural and constructed world, performing and evaluating investigations and communicating their findings. These principles should guide student work and be integrated into the curriculum along with the content standards on a daily basis.

Lesson **1**

Essential Question

How Do We Use Inquiry Skills?

Engage Your Brain!

Find the answer in this lesson.

You tell how these flowers are alike and different.

You are ___comparing___ them.

Active Reading

Lesson Vocabulary

1. Preview the lesson.

2. Write the vocabulary term here.

___Inquiry skills___

Use Inquiry Skills

Inquiry skills help people find out information. Inquiry skills help people plan and do tests.

These children use inquiry skills to do a task for school. They are observing. Observe means to use your five senses to learn about things.

Active Reading

Find the sentence that tells the meaning of **observe**. Draw a line under the sentence.

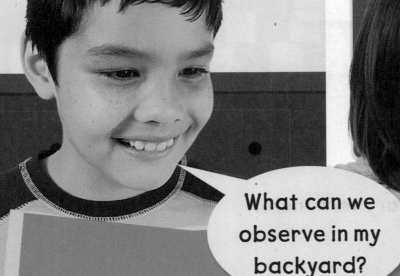

What can we observe in my backyard?

Danny and Sophie want to observe things in the backyard. They (plan an investigation). They plan how to find out what they want to know. They also (predict), or make a good guess, about what they will (observe).

► This page names three (inquiry skills). Circle the name for one of the (skills).

Explore the Backyard

Danny and Sophie head out to the backyard to begin their task. Danny finds the length and the height of the birdhouse. He measures it with a ruler.

They use inquiry skills to learn more about the backyard.

Sophie compares leaves. She observes how they are alike and how they are different. She may also classify, or sort, many leaves in the backyard by the way they are alike.

▶ Look at Sophie's leaves.
Put them in order of size from smallest to largest.

2   1   3

Model and Infer

Now Danny and Sophie draw a map of the backyard. <u>They are making a model to show what something is like.</u> You could also make a model to show how something works.

My Backyard

birch tree

rose bush

maple tree

bird bath

bird house

Active Reading

Find the sentences that explain what it means to **make a model**. Draw a line under the sentences.

Danny and Sophie use one more inquiry skill. They infer. They use what they know to answer a question—Are there any living things in the backyard? They can infer that the backyard is home to many plants and animals.

▶ Think about what you know about winter. Infer what Danny and Sophie might observe in the backyard during winter.

They observe snow, no leaves on the tree, and icesicls.

Sum It Up!

① Complete It!

Fill in the blank.

How are measuring, observing, and predicting alike?

They are all

_____ .

② Circle It!

Circle the skill name to match the meaning.

Which one means to choose steps you will do to learn something?

infer

plan an investigation

classify

③ Draw and Write It!

Observe something outside. Then draw and write to record your observations.

_____

_____

 **Brain Check**

Name _____

Word Play

Read each clue below. Then unscramble the letters to write the correct answer.

observe	compare	measure	infer

1 to find the size or amount of something

s e m a r e u _____

2 to use your senses to learn about something

b o s r e e v _____

3 to observe how things are alike and different

p o c r a m e _____

4 to use what you know to answer a question

f n i r e _____

Apply Concepts

Match each inquiry skill to its meaning.

| to make a good guess about what will happen | plan an investigation |

| to sort things by how they are alike | classify |

| to show what something is like or how it works | predict |

| to follow steps to answer a question | make a model |

Take It Home!

Family Members: Work with your child to measure two objects in your home. Have your child compare the two objects and tell which is larger.

Essential Question

How Do We Use Science Tools?

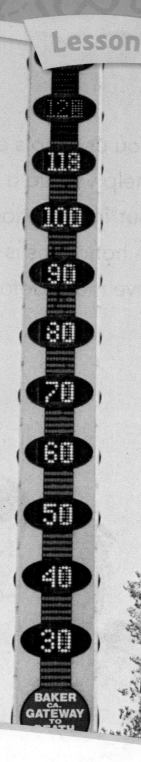

Engage Your Brain!

Find the answer to the question in the lesson.

What does a thermometer measure?

_____

Active Reading

Lesson Vocabulary

1. Preview the lesson.

2. Write the 2 vocabulary terms here.

_____   _____

Top Tools

You use tools every day. Tools are things that help you do a job. **Science tools** help you find out information.

A hand lens is one science tool. It helps you observe more details than with your eyes alone.

What can you see through this hand lens? Circle it.

A hand lens makes things look larger.

Measuring Tools

You use some tools for measuring things. You use a **thermometer** to measure temperature. You use a measuring cup to measure amounts of liquids.

Active Reading

The main idea is the most important idea about something. Draw a line under the main idea on this page.

A thermometer measures temperature in units called degrees.

A measuring cup measures liquids in units called milliliters, cups, and ounces.

15

Measure More!

You use a tool called a scale to measure weight. You can use a balance to measure mass.

This scale measures weight in units called pounds and ounces.

> ▶ Name two things you can weigh on a scale.
>
> _____
>
> _____

This balance measures mass in units called grams and kilograms.

You use a ruler and a tape measure to measure distance as well as length, width, and height. Both tools measure in units called inches or centimeters.

▶ Circle the object the ruler is measuring.

A ruler measures objects with straight lines.

A tape measure can measure around an object.

17

Sum It Up!

① Answer It!

Write the answer to this question.

You want to measure how much water fits into a pail. What tool could you use?

_____

② Draw It!

Draw yourself using a measuring tool.

③ Mark It!

Mark an X on the tool that does <u>not</u> measure.

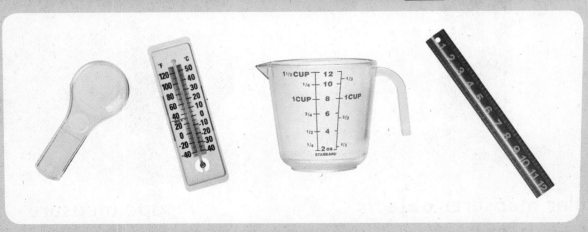

Name _____

Word Play

Match the name of each tool to its picture.

tape measure	
balance	
thermometer	
measuring cup	
hand lens	

Apply Concepts

Name the tool you could use for each job.

measuring the length of a book	_____
finding the weight of a watermelon	_____
observing curves and lines on the tip of your finger	_____

Take It Home!

Family Members: Go on a scavenger hunt. See which tools from this lesson you have in or around your home. Discuss with your child how to use each tool.

Name _____

The Nature of Science Students gain scientific knowledge by observing the natural and constructed world, performing and evaluating investigations and communicating their findings. These principles should guide student work and be integrated into the curriculum along with the content standards on a daily basis.

Essential Question

What Tools Can We Use?

Set a Purpose

Write what you want to find out.

_____

_____

Think About the Procedure

1 Which science tool did you choose? What does it do?

_____

_____

2 How will the tool help you observe the object?

_____

_____

Record Your Data

Record your observations in this chart.

My Object _____	
My Tool _____	
What I Learned Without the Tool	What I Learned With the Tool

Draw Conclusions

How can a science tool help you learn more about an object?

_____

_____

_____

Ask More Questions

What other questions can you ask about how science tools are used?

_____

_____

_____

Essential Question

How Do Scientists Think?

Engage Your Brain!

Find the answer in the lesson.

When scientists _____ they follow steps and use tools to answer a question.

Active Reading

Lesson Vocabulary

1 Preview the lesson.

2 Write the 4 vocabulary terms here.

_____   _____

_____   _____

Let's Observe It!

Scientists **investigate**. They plan and do a test to answer a question or solve a problem. They use inquiry skills and science tools to help them.

There are many ways to investigate. But many scientists follow a sequence, or order of events. Here's one possible sequence. First, scientists may observe and ask a question.

Active Reading

Clue words can help you find the order of things. **First** is a clue word. Circle this clue word in the paragraph above.

Does food coloring spread faster in cold water or warm water?

cold

Now, scientists can make a hypothesis. A **hypothesis** is a statement that can be tested. Then scientists plan a fair test. The scientists list the materials they will need and the steps they will take to do their test.

Food coloring spreads faster in warm water.

food coloring

warm

Let's Test It!

Next, the scientists are ready to do their test. They follow their plan and record what they observe.

Active Reading

Clue words can help you find the order of things. **Next** is a clue word. Circle this clue word in the paragraph above.

These children test whether food coloring spreads faster in cold water or warm water.

After the test, scientists **draw conclusions**. They use the information they have gathered to decide if their results support the hypothesis. Finally, they write or draw to **communicate** what they learned.

▶ How does the temperature of water affect how fast the food coloring spreads? Draw a conclusion.

_____

_____

_____

▶ What else could a scientist test with water and food coloring?

_____

_____

_____

warm

Let's Check Again!

Scientists do the same test a few times. They need to make sure that they get similar results every time. In this investigation, the food coloring should spread faster in warm water every time.

Our Food Colori

cold   warm   cold   warm

Monday   Wednesday

► Look at the **warm** cup for both Monday and Friday. Draw a conclusion. Color in the **warm** cup for Wednesday to show what it should look like.

Test

cold

warm

Friday

Do the Math!
Measure Length

Choose an object. Use a ruler to measure the object's length. Measure it three times. Record.

Length of _____	
Measure 1	
Measure 2	
Measure 3	

1. How do your numbers compare?

_____

_____

2. Why do you think so?

_____

_____

_____

Sum It Up!

① Order It!

Number the steps from 1 to 4 to tell a way scientists investigate.

_____ Observe and ask a question.

_____ Do the test and record what happens.

_____ Draw conclusions and communicate.

_____ Make a hypothesis and plan a fair test.

② Circle It!

Circle the correct answer.

Suppose you make a poster to show the results of your test. You are _____.

observing   planning your test

making a hypothesis   communicating

Word Play

Circle the word to complete each sentence.

1. You use inquiry skills and science tools to learn. You _____.

   communicate   investigate

2. You take the first step to do an investigation. You _____.

   draw conclusions   observe

3. You make a statement that you can test. You make a _____.

   hypothesis   conclusion

4. You use information you gathered to explain what you learned. You _____.

   draw conclusions   observe

5. You write to tell about the results of a test. You _____.

   communicate   ask a question

Apply Concepts

These steps show a test some children did.
Label each box with a step from this lesson.

The children look at an ice cube. They ask—
Will it melt in the sun?

Observe and _____.

They form a statement that the ice cube will melt in the sun.

_____.

They follow their plan. The ice cube melts! They decide that the sun's heat caused the ice to melt.

Test and _____.

The children write and draw to tell the results of their test.

_____.

Take It Home!

Family Members: Work with your child to plan an investigation. Use the steps from this lesson.

Name _____

The Nature of Science Students gain scientific knowledge by observing the natural and constructed world, performing and evaluating investigations and communicating their findings. These principles should guide student work and be integrated into the curriculum along with the content standards on a daily basis.

Essential Question

How Do We Solve a Problem?

Set a Purpose

What problem do you want to solve?

_____

_____

Think About the Procedure

❶ Why do you make a list of the properties the holder must have?

_____

_____

❷ Why do you design your holder before you build it?

_____

_____

Record Your Data

Record the details of your plan in this chart.

The Problem	
My Plan	
Materials I need	

Draw Conclusions

Sometimes it is helpful to make a model first before making the real thing. How can making a model help you solve a problem?

_____

_____

Ask More Questions

What other questions do you have about designing and making models to solve problems?

_____

_____

4 Things to Know About Anders Celsius

1

In 1742, Celsius invented the Celsius scale to measure temperature.

2

The temperature at which water freezes on the Celsius scale is 0°.

3

The temperature at which water boils on the Celsius scale is 100°.

4

Celsius was an astronomer, or a person who studies the stars and other things in space.

Celsius Match Up

1

▶ **Read each thermometer. Write the number that matches the correct temperature in each picture.**

2

3

▶ How does a temperature scale help you tell about the weather?

_____

_____

Multiple Choice
Fill in the circle next to the best answer.

Nature of Science

1 Jared knows that his two blocks are the same color but different shapes. How does he know?

- ○ He measures them.
- ○ He observes and compares them.
- ○ He makes a model.

Nature of Science

2 Gail uses this tool to find the length of a book.

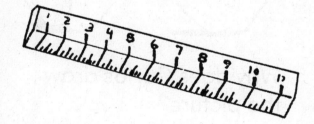

What is she doing?
- ○ classifying
- ○ inferring
- ○ measuring

Nature of Science

3 Victor uses a scale to measure the weight of a melon. He observes that the melon weighs three pounds. Ana also uses a scale to measure the weight of the same melon. What should Ana observe?

- ○ The melon weighs two pounds.
- ○ The melon weighs three pounds.
- ○ The melon weighs four pounds.

Nature of Science

4 Lea investigates to answer a question. Then she repeats her experiment several times. Which will MOST LIKELY be true?

○ The results will be the same.

○ The results will be different.

○ She cannot compare the results.

Nature of Science

5 Sumeet looks at the sky before he goes to school. It is dark and cloudy outside. What skill is Sumeet using?

○ comparing

○ inferring

○ observing

Nature of Science

6 How do scientists work to solve problems?

○ They solve problems the same way each time.

○ They always work alone.

○ They keep looking for new ways to solve problems.

Nature of Science

7 Carlos completes an investigation. He draws this picture in a notebook.

Why does Carlos draw the picture?

○ to plan the investigation

○ to predict what will happen

○ to record what he observed

Nature of Science

8 You think that an ant and a butterfly have the same parts. Why would making a model of both insects be a good way to find out if this is true?

○ The models would show parts that the real insects have.

○ The models would be the same size as the real insects.

○ Making the models would mean that you do not have to make observations.

Nature of Science

9 Gina observes the temperature in the morning. She wants to find out how the afternoon temperature compares to the morning temperature. What should she do to find out?

○ Infer the afternoon temperature. Then compare it to the morning temperature.

○ Measure the afternoon temperature. Then compare it to the morning temperature.

○ Predict the afternoon temperature. Then compare it to the morning temperature.

Nature of Science

10 Antonio wants to find out how much water and sunlight plants need to grow. What should he do FIRST?

○ measure the plants
○ plan an investigation
○ record his results

Nature of Science

11 Christine wants to observe details of the flower.

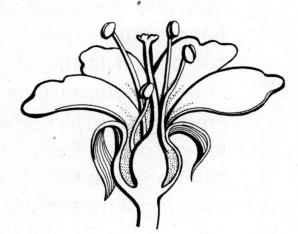

Which tool should she use?

○ a hand lens
○ a ruler
○ a scale

Nature of Science

12 Tess wants to know whether a tree or a bush is taller. Which tool should she use?

○ a balance
○ a hand lens
○ a tape measure

Nature of Science

13 Which tool can you use to measure weight?

○

○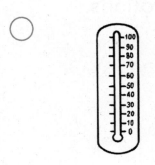

○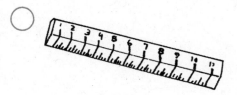

Nature of Science

14 What can you observe about a leaf by using a hand lens?

- ○ how the leaf makes food
- ○ how the leaf feels
- ○ the leaf's shape and color

Nature of Science

15 Which is TRUE about an investigation?

- ○ All scientists follow the same steps in an investigation.
- ○ There are many ways to investigate a question.
- ○ There is only one correct way to investigate a question.

Nature of Science

16 You complete an investigation about plants. Now you have another question. What should you do?

- ○ do a test
- ○ plan a new investigation
- ○ repeat the same investigation

Nature of Science

17 How is this boy using the tool?

- ○ He is weighing himself.
- ○ He is weighing the fruit.
- ○ He is measuring the length of the fruit.

Nature of Science

18 What do you do when you draw a conclusion?

○ tell what you want to learn from a test

○ tell what you think will happen during a test

○ form an idea about what you learned from a test

Nature of Science

19 Which is an example of making a model?

○ building a clay volcano to see how a volcano works

○ measuring temperature

○ planting seeds to see how plants grow

Nature of Science

20 Which is TRUE?

○ You build a model before you draw a design.

○ You draw a design and build a model at the same time.

○ You draw a design before you build a model.

Matter

a stream in Indiana

I Wonder Why

Ice has formed on this stream. Why?
Turn the page to find out.

Here's Why The liquid water in the stream turns to solid ice when it gets very cold.

Track Your Progress

Essential Questions and Indiana Standards

STANDARD 1
Physical Science

Observe and describe that the properties of materials can change, but not all materials respond in the same way to the same action.

2.1.1. Observe, describe, and measure ways in which the properties of a sample of water (including volume) change or stay the same as it is heated and cooled and is transformed into different states.

Essential Question

What Are Solids, Liquids, and Gases?

Engage Your Brain!

Find the answer to the question in the lesson.

What is inside the balloon?

_____

Active Reading

Lesson Vocabulary

1 Preview the lesson.

2 Write the 8 vocabulary terms here.

_____   _____

_____   _____

_____   _____

_____   _____

Matter Matters

The boy and the objects around him are matter. **Matter** takes up space and has mass. **Mass** is the amount of matter in an object.

Solid, liquid, and gas are three states of matter. The boy's sunglasses are a solid. The water in his bottle is a liquid. The beach ball is filled with gases.

Active Reading

Find the sentence that tells the meaning of **mass**. Draw a line under the sentence.

What two states of matter make up the beach ball?

Solid as a Rock

Look at the chair, the towel, and the hat. How are these objects the same? The answer is that all three are solids.

A **solid** is the only state of matter that has its own shape. What other solids do you see in this picture?

▶ Draw a solid object that you would take to the beach.

Shape Up!

Is juice a solid? No. It does not have its own shape. If you pour juice from a pitcher into a glass, the shape of the juice changes.

Juice is a liquid. A **liquid** is a state of matter that takes the shape of its container. What other liquids can you name?

▶ Color the empty glass to show the shape the liquid would take in it.

Salt water is a kind of liquid.

Life's a Gas

This girl is blowing air into the beach ball. Air is made up of gases. A **gas** is a state of matter that fills all the space in its container. The air will keep spreading out until it fills the entire beach ball.

Active Reading

Find the sentence that tells the meaning of **gas**. Draw a line under the sentence.

You can't see air, but you can see and feel what it does.

Wonderful Water

On the outside of this glass, water vapor is becoming liquid water.

You can't see it, but water vapor is in the air around this glass.

There are three states of water—solid, liquid, and gas. The water we drink is a liquid. Solid water is ice. Water in the form of a gas is **water vapor**.

▶ What is water vapor?

_____

_____

States of Water

Write in each empty box to complete the chart.

Name	State	Shape
ice	solid	_____
water	_____	takes the shape of its container
_____	gas	fills up all the space in a container

Deep Freeze

Taking away or adding heat can change water. Think about making ice. Put water in the freezer. The water freezes into solid ice. Take the ice out of the freezer. It melts into a liquid.

Freezing changes some properties of water. Ice has its own shape. Liquid water does not. Freezing makes water expand. So ice takes up more space than water.

Active Reading

The main idea is the most important idea about something. Draw a line under the main idea.

An ice pop is mostly water. Here it is frozen solid.

▶ Draw something that melts.

© Houghton Mifflin Harcourt Publishing Company (bkgd) ©Getty Images/PhotoDisc

The ice pop gets warm and melts into a liquid.

Do the Math!
Compare Numbers

Circle the answers.

Ice cream has a lot of water in it. It melts faster when the air temperature is higher.

At which temperature will ice cream melt faster?

75 °F **or** 45 °F

50 °F **or** 85 °F

Adding and Subtracting

Adding heat can change water. Look at the water in the pot. How does it change as the stove heats it? The water turns into water vapor. It evaporates into the air. **Evaporation** is the change of water from a liquid to a gas.

Active Reading

Find the sentence that tells the meaning of **evaporation**. Draw a line under the sentence.

evaporation

condensation

How does water vapor change back into water? Just take away heat. Look at the water on the window. The cold window cools water vapor in the air. The water vapor changes to water. It condenses as water drops on the window. **Condensation** is the change of water from a gas to a liquid.

▶ Circle each math term that helps you understand evaporation and condensation.

Sum It Up!

① Match It!

Draw lines to match each object with its state of matter.

solid

liquid

gas

② Circle It!

Circle the answer.

What happens when you heat liquid water?

evaporation
condensation

_____

What happens when you freeze water?

It shrinks.
It expands.

③ Write It!

Answer the question.

What are the three states of water?

_____

Name _____

Word Play

Write the word for each clue. Fill in the missing numbers in the table. Then decode the message.

A	B	C	D	E	F	G	H	I	J	K	L	M
	26			25		13		6	14		5	

N	O	P	Q	R	S	T	U	V	W	X	Y	Z
									10	2	19	24

takes the shape of its container

$\overline{20}\ \overline{23}\ \overline{3}\ \overline{4}\ \overline{23}\ \overline{16}$

water in the form of a gas

$\overline{15}\ \overline{11}\ \overline{1}\ \overline{18}\ \overline{22}$

when gas turns to liquid

$\overline{12}\ \overline{18}\ \overline{17}\ \overline{16}\ \overline{8}\ \overline{17}\ \overline{21}\ \overline{11}\ \overline{9}\ \overline{23}\ \overline{18}\ \overline{17}$

fills all the space of its container

$\overline{7}\ \overline{11}\ \overline{21}$

$\overline{11}\quad\overline{16}\ \overline{11}\ \overline{19}\quad\overline{11}\ \overline{9}\quad\overline{9}\ \overline{13}\ \overline{8}$

$\overline{26}\ \overline{8}\ \overline{11}\ \overline{12}\ \overline{13}\quad\overline{23}\ \overline{21}\quad\overline{11}$

$\overline{20}\ \overline{11}\ \overline{4}\ \overline{7}\ \overline{13}\ \overline{23}\ \overline{17}\ \overline{7}\quad\overline{5}\ \overline{11}\ \overline{9}\ \overline{9}\ \overline{8}\ \overline{22}$!

Write or draw to fill in the chart with examples of solids, liquids, and gases.

Solids, Liquids, and Gases

Solids	Liquids	Gases

Take It Home!

Family Members: Walk around your home with your child, and point out objects and materials. Ask your child to classify each one as a solid, a liquid, or a gas.

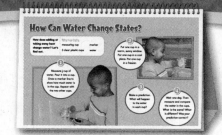

2.1.1. Observe, describe, and measure ways in which the properties of a sample of water (including volume) change or stay the same as it is heated and cooled and is transformed into different states.

Name _____

Essential Question

How Can Water Change States?

Set a Purpose

Tell what you want to find out in this investigation.

Will the amount of water change in a cup when we freeze ~~the~~ water

Make Predictions

What do you think will happen to the water?

Freeze-get cold or freeze

~~Room~~ cold get to the room temp

~~Heat~~ room get warm or hot

Think About the Procedure

Why do you measure the water at the beginning of the activity?
Why do you measure again at the end?

So you can see thee amount of

change.

Record Your Data

Record the amount of water at the start. At the end, record your observations and measurements as possible.

	Warm Place	Cool Place	Freezer
Start	W	C	F
End	W	C	F

Draw Conclusions

Were your predictions correct? How does adding heat and taking away heat affect water?

Not all of my prediction were rite. Adding heat will make water evaporate. If you take away

Ask More Questions

What other questions could you ask about the ways water can change?

Essential Question

What Are Some Ways to Change Matter?

Engage Your Brain!

Find the answer to the question in the lesson.

How were the foods changed to make the giraffe?

_____

Active Reading

Lesson Vocabulary

1 Preview the lesson.

2 Write the 3 vocabulary terms here.

_____   _____

_____

Make a Change

A carrot is long, thin, and orange. These words tell about the carrot's size, shape, and color. Size, shape, and color are properties. A **property** is one part of what something is like. All matter has properties.

You can change the properties of matter. Cutting, folding, tearing, and breaking can change properties.

Active Reading

A cause tells why something happens. Circle words that name actions that cause changes to properties of matter.

cutting

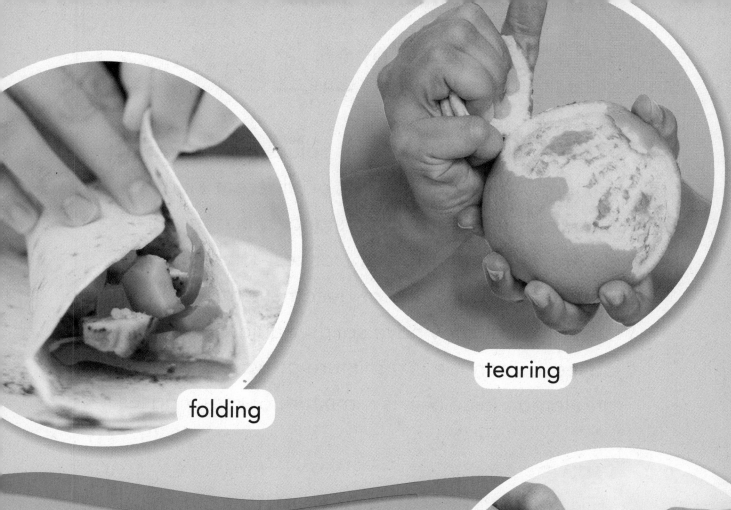

folding

tearing

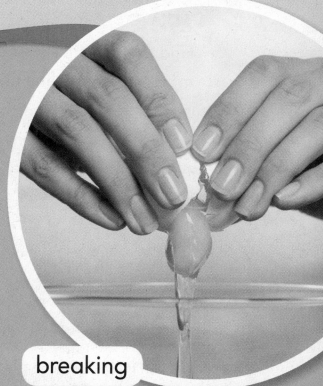

breaking

▶ Think of a food. Draw a way you can change it.

Mix and Match

The girl is making fruit salad. Fruit salad is a mixture. A **mixture** is a mix of different kinds of matter. The things, or substances, in a mixture do not become other substances. The fruits in the salad mix but do not become other things.

Mixtures may have solids, liquids, and gases. Lemonade is a mixture of water, sugar, and lemon juice. Air is a mixture of many gases.

Active Reading

Find the sentence that tells the meaning of **mixture**. Draw a line under that sentence.

strawberry

orange

grape

pineapple

▶ Label each part of the fruit salad.
Then tell why it is a mixture.

_____

_____

_____

_____

_____

Time for a Change

When matter is cut or broken, its size and shape change. Matter also changes when it **dissolves**, or mixes completely with a liquid. Dissolving can change the properties of matter.

Sugar, for example, dissolves in water. It spreads out and seems to disappear. The properties of the sugar change.

Changes to Matter

▶ Circle **yes** or **no** to answer the questions in each row.

Can you dissolve it in water?

lemonade powder and sugar

yes   no

Can you cut it?

apple

yes   no

Can you break it?

egg

yes   no

salt

yes   **no**

spoon

yes   **no**

ruler

yes   **no**

paper

yes   **no**

crayon

yes   **no**

eraser

yes   **no**

Change to Chew On

When you prepare food, you change matter. Think about making a salad. You tear lettuce. You cut tomatoes. You mix oil and vinegar for dressing. You may dissolve salt in the dressing, too. You combine the solid vegetables and the liquid dressing. Some properties of the foods change. Some stay the same. But the mixture tastes great!

How have cooks changed matter in the mixtures you see here?

taco salad

fruit salad

© Houghton Mifflin Harcourt Publishing Company (bkgd) ©C Squared Studios/Getty Images/PhotoDisc; (cf) ©Foodcollection/AGE Fotostock; (bl) ©Lew Robertson/Brand X/Corbis

pasta salad

green salad

▶ Write about a dish you like to make. Tell all the ways you change matter.

_____

Sum It Up!

① Write It!

Write two ways you can change matter.

_____

_____

_____

_____

② Circle It!

Circle the word that best describes the picture.

mixture   dissolve

③ Mark It!

Mark an X on each thing that dissolves in water.

 **Brain Check**

Name _____

Word Play

Draw lines through the maze. Match each word at the top with its picture at the bottom.

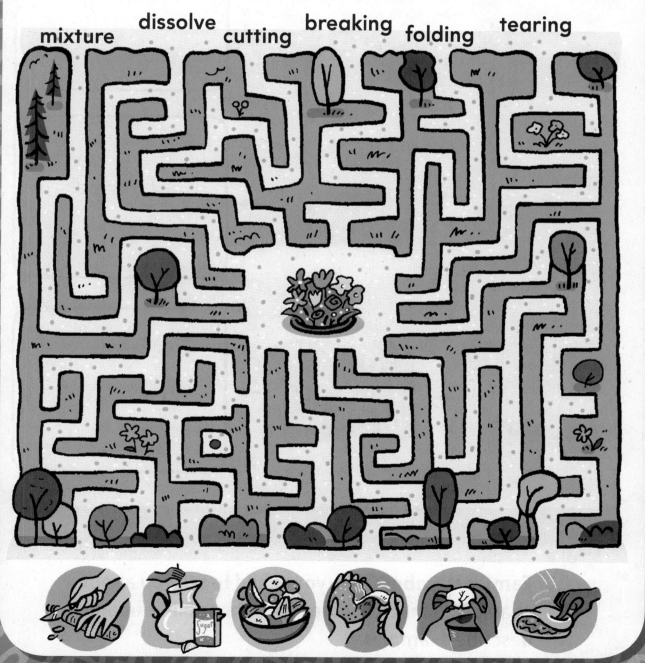

mixture   dissolve   cutting   breaking   folding   tearing

In each box, write to explain how the property of the matter has changed.

Cause   **Effect**

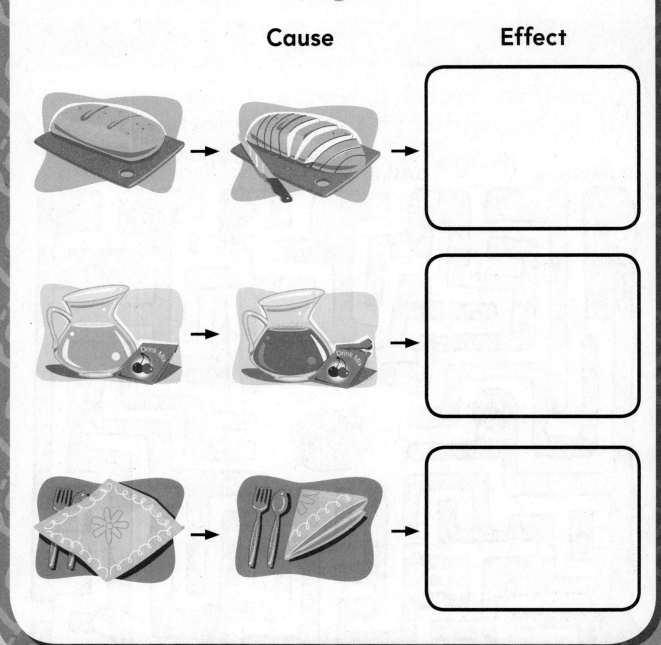

Family Members: Ask your child to tell you about changes to matter. Have him or her point out and describe examples.

Take It Home!

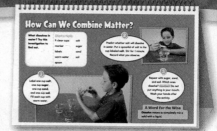

2.1.2. Predict the result of combining solids and liquids in pairs. Mix; observe, gather, record and discuss evidence that the result may be a material with different properties than the original materials.

Name _____

Essential Question

How Can We Combine Matter?

Set a Purpose

Tell what you will do in this investigation.

_____

_____

Make a Prediction

Which substances will dissolve? Write your prediction.

_____

_____

Think About the Procedure

How do you know when something dissolves in water?

_____

_____

Record Your Data

Record your observations in this chart.

Substance	Did It Dissolve?	How Are Properties Different?
Salt		
Sand		
Soil		
Sugar		

Draw Conclusions

Were your predictions correct?

_____

_____

Do all things dissolve in water? Explain.

_____

_____

Ask More Questions

What other questions can you ask about dissolving?

_____

_____

2.1.3. Predict and experiment with methods (e.g. sieving, evaporation) to separate solids and liquids based on their physical properties.

Name _____

Essential Question

How Can We Separate Matter?

Set a Purpose

Tell what you want to do.

_____

Think About the Procedure

1 How could you separate the rice from the water?

_____

_____

2 How could you separate the salt from the water?

_____

_____

3 Predict the best way to separate rice and salt from the water.

_____

_____

Record Your Data

Record each idea you tried and what happened.

What I Tried	What Happened

Draw Conclusions

Was your prediction correct? What worked best to separate salt and rice from the water?

_____

_____

_____

Ask More Questions

What other questions could you ask about separating matter?

_____

_____

_____

2.4.2 Identify technologies developed by humans to meet a human need and investigate the limitations of the technology and how it has improved quality of life. **Nature of Science**

People in Science

Get to Know...
Dr. Mario Molina

Dr. Mario Molina is a chemist, or a person who studies the properties of substances and how they interact. For many years he studied materials called chlorofluorocarbons (CFCs). CFCs were used in spray cans and refrigerators. Dr. Molina found that CFCs harm the ozone layer, a layer of gas around Earth. The ozone layer protects us from the sun's harmful rays.

Fun Fact

When Dr. Molina was a boy, he used a microscope to look at very tiny living things like this one.

77

This Leads to That

Dr. Molina and other scientists talked to lawmakers. They worked to get rid of CFCs in spray cans.

Now the ozone layer is coming back, thanks to Dr. Molina and others. In 1995, Dr. Molina won the Nobel Prize for his work.

▶ How did Dr. Molina's work help the environment?

_____

_____

Multiple Choice
Fill in the circle next to the best answer.

Nature of Science

1 Which object is a solid?
- ○ a penny
- ○ a puddle
- ○ a raindrop

2.1.1

2 Which is TRUE about ice?
- ○ It takes up more space than the same amount of water.
- ○ It takes up less space than the same amount of water.
- ○ It takes up the same space as the same amount of water.

2.1.1

3 Shane has some ice cubes in a glass. What state of matter are the ice cubes?
- ○ gas
- ○ liquid
- ○ solid

2.1.1

4 On Friday, Rashad measures how much water fills a water bottle. He observes that it holds 3 cups. On Sunday, he measures how much water fills the same bottle. How much water does the bottle hold on Sunday?
- ○ 2 cups
- ○ 3 cups
- ○ 4 cups

Nature of Science

5 Which of these can you cut with scissors?

○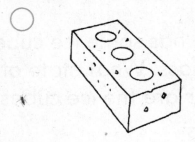

○

○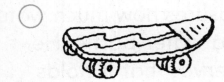

2.1.2

6 What happens when you mix and stir salt into water?

○ It dissolves.

○ It freezes.

○ It melts.

2.1.2

7 Ian stirs sand into a glass of warm water. He knows the sand is not dissolving in the water. How does he know?

○ All the sand sinks to the bottom of the glass.

○ The sand spreads out and mixes completely with the water.

○ The sand melts in the water.

2.1.1

8 Which picture shows water in a solid state?

○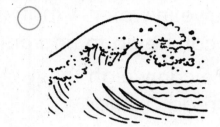

○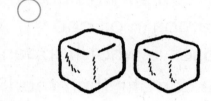

○

2.1.1

9 How does water change as a stove heats it?

○ It becomes ice.

○ It doesn't change.

○ It turns into water vapor.

2.1.1

10 Which is an example of water in a liquid state?

○ an ice skating rink

○ a river

○ water vapor

Nature of Science

11 How did the plate change?

○ It broke.

○ It dissolved.

○ It melted.

2.1.1

12 Which will become solid in a freezer?

○ a glass plate
○ juice
○ a metal nail

2.1.2

13 Which dissolves in water?

○ marbles
○ rocks
○ sugar

Nature of Science

14 Pat is having a sandwich. How is she changing the shape of the sandwich?

○ She is cutting it.
○ She is folding it.
○ She is melting it.

2.1.2

15 Jin wants to find out whether bread crumbs dissolve in water. What test can he do to find out?

○ He can weigh the bread crumbs.
○ He can stir the bread crumbs in oil and observe what happens.
○ He can stir the bread crumbs in water and observe what happens.

2.1.2

16 What is a mix of different kinds of matter?

○ a gas
○ a mixture
○ a property

2.1.3

17 You put a glass of water in a warm place. You observe the water again the next day. What do you observe about the water?

 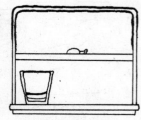

Monday, 6:00 A.M.   Tuesday, 6:00 A.M.

○ Some of the water has evaporated.

○ The water is exactly the same.

○ There is more water in the glass.

2.1.3

18 The sun comes out after a winter storm. Which part of the snowman will melt?

○ the carrot nose

○ the body made of snow

○ the hat

2.1.3

19 Mr. Lewis cooks potatoes in water. He uses a large sieve to separate the potatoes from the water. What happens?

○ The potatoes dissolve.

○ Water drains through the sieve.

○ The potatoes drain through the sieve.

2.1.3

20 What is this woman doing?

○ She is freezing water.

○ She is using a container to hold water.

○ She is using a sieve to separate shells from the water.

Motion and Forces

STANDARD 1
Physical Science

Indianapolis Colts kicker

I Wonder Why

The ball changes position when the kicker kicks it. Why?

Turn the page to find out.

Here's Why The ball changes position because of the force from the kicker's foot.

Track Your Progress

Essential Questions and Indiana Standards

STANDARD 1
Physical Science

Observe and describe the motion of an object and how it changes when a force is applied to it.

Essential Question

How Do Objects Move?

Engage Your Brain!

Find the answer to the question in the lesson.

These Ferris wheel lights look blurry when they are in motion.

How does this Ferris wheel move?

_____

Active Reading

Lesson Vocabulary

1 Preview the lesson.

2 Write the 2 vocabulary terms here.

_____   _____

Set Things in Motion

The log ride climbs up the hill slowly.

log ride

Look at all of the things in motion! **Motion** is movement. When something is in motion, it is moving.

Planes fly fast. A turtle walks slowly. **Speed** is the measure of how fast something moves.

▶ Circle two things that move fast. Mark Xs on two things that move slowly.

Do the Math!

Make a Bar Graph

Pam went on three rides. This graph shows how long she waited for each ride.

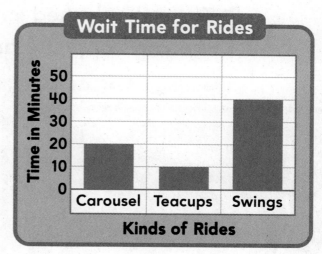

Wait Time for Rides

Time in Minutes
50
40
30
20
10
0

Carousel Teacups Swings

Kinds of Rides

Use the graph to answer the questions.

1. Which ride had the shortest wait time?

_____

2. How does the graph tell you?

_____

_____

The log ride zooms down the hill fast.

It's Your Move!

Objects can move in many ways.
They can move in a straight line, zigzag, back and forth, or round and round.

▶ Trace the dashed lines below to show the ways objects can move.

This roller coaster is moving in a straight line down the track.

A bumper car can zigzag from place to place.

A detail is a fact about a main idea. Draw one line under a detail. Draw an arrow to the main idea it tells about.

This ship ride swings back and forth.

A Ferris wheel spins round and round.

Sum It Up!

1 Draw It!

Read the label in each box. Draw an arrow to show the kind of motion.

back and forth	zigzag	round and round	straight line

2 Circle It!

Look at each pair of objects. Circle the one that goes faster.

92

Name _____

Word Play

Work your way through the maze to match the word with its meaning.

Apply Concepts

Complete the word web below. In each circle,
write one way things move. Then give an example.

The Way Things Move

zigzag

_____

example—

_____

bumper car

_____

_____

_____

_____

motion

_____

_____

_____

_____

Take It Home!

Family Members: Ask your child to tell you about how
objects move. Point out objects in motion. Have your
child talk about the motion and speed of the objects.

2.1.4 Observe, sketch, demonstrate, and compare how objects can move in different ways (straight, zig-zag, back-and-forth, rolling, fast and slow).

Name _____

Essential Question

How Can We Move a Ball?

Set a Purpose

Tell what you will do in this investigation.

_____

Think About the Procedure

1 What kinds of motions will you show?

_____

_____

2 How will you show the motion?

_____

_____

_____

Record Your Data

Draw what you did.

Motion	Drawing
Straight line	
Zigzag	
Back and forth	
Round and round	

Draw Conclusions

1 How are all the motions the same?

_____

_____

2 How are the motions of the ball different?

_____

Ask More Questions

What other questions can you ask about how objects move?

_____

_____

96

2.1.5 Describe the position or motion of an object relative to a point of reference (background or another object). **2.1.6** Observe, sketch, demonstrate, and compare how applied force (push or pull) changes the motion of objects.

Lesson **3**

Essential Question

How Can We Change the Way Objects Move?

Engage Your Brain!

Find the answer to the question in the lesson.

How is pushing a swing like pulling a wagon?

A push and a pull are both

_____

Active Reading

Lesson Vocabulary

1 Preview the lesson.

2 Write the 5 vocabulary terms here.

_____ _____ _____

_____ _____

In Full Force

What makes the wagon move? The girl gives it a push. A **push** presses an object away from you. The boy gives the wagon a pull. A **pull** tugs an object closer to you.

Pushes and pulls are forces. A **force** makes an object move or stop moving. When the girl and boy push and pull the wagon, it moves.

▶ **Draw yourself pushing something.**

▶ Draw yourself pulling something.

Active Reading

Find the sentence that tells the meaning of **force**. Draw a line under the sentence.

Using Force

Look at the pictures. How does a force move a ball? A force can change the way an object moves. It can change a ball's speed or direction.

Changing Speed

Force can change an object's speed. It can make something start moving or stop moving. It can make something go faster or more slowly.

▶ What is going to happen to the ball?

_____

_____

You can kick a ball to make it start moving or go faster.

You can catch
a ball to stop it.

▶ Describe how the motion of the car changes.

1

2

3

1 _____

2 _____

3 _____

What Is Your Position?

The **position** of an object tells where it is located. Use position words to tell where an object is or where it is moving to. Some position words are **in, out, up, down, above, below, in front of, behind, left,** and **right.**

Active Reading

A detail is a fact about a main idea. Draw one line under a detail. Draw an arrow to the main idea it tells about.

The sand is moving **down** into the bucket.

The sand is **up above** the bucket.

The shells are **in** the bucket.

The shells are **out** of the bucket.

A Step in the Right Direction

Think about pushing someone on a swing. The person moves away from you and then comes back. A force can change the direction of an object. The **direction** of an object is the path the object moves along. Forces can move things toward you and away from you.

▶ Tell how the direction of this swing changes.

_____

_____

What Makes That Coaster Move?

A roller coaster is fun! It goes up and down, fast and slow, round and round. People on the ride might yell as it changes speed and direction. What makes the coaster move?

Different forces make a roller coaster move. A motor pulls a chain. The chain pulls the car up the first hill.

Gravity is the force that pulls the car down. Gravity pulls all things toward Earth. The speed of the car changes as it moves down. It moves faster.

▶ **What pulls the car down the hill?**

_____

Sum It Up!

① Solve It!

Write the word that solves the riddle.

I move a box

  when it is full.

I can be

  a push or a pull.

    What am I?

_____

② Circle It!

Forces can change motion. Circle the words that tell the kinds of changes.

speed	color
size	direction
shape	position

③ Label It!

Write <u>push</u> or <u>pull</u> to label each picture.

_____   _____

Word Play

Complete the story by using these words.

speed	push	force	pull	direction	position

Dear Jen,

We moved into our new house. My dad drove the moving truck. He made sure the _____ of the truck was not too fast. Dad drove away from our old house. He went along the road in the _____ of our new house.

Moving is hard! I had to _____ boxes all day. It took a huge _____ to move my box of toys. My dad had to _____ it while my brother pushed. Then we had to move the boxes up and down the stairs. Changing the _____ of those boxes took work!

Your friend,

Amy

Apply Concepts

Complete the chart. Write a word on each blank line.

Cause	Effect
Force	moves a _____.
Force	makes a wagon go _____.
Force	pushes a swing _____ from you.
Force	moves a book to a new _____ on a shelf.

Take It Home!

Family Members: Ask your child to tell you about forces and motion. Have your child point out examples of pushes and pulls, and explain how those forces change motion.

1

He is known for observing an apple falling from a tree.

2

He wrote his Three Laws of Motion.

4

Things to Know About

Isaac Newton

3

His laws help us understand why things move the way they do.

4

He was one of the greatest scientists in history.

Objects in Motion

▶ Think about what you know about Isaac Newton. Then write the answer to each question.

What did Isaac Newton write after seeing an apple fall from a tree?

_____

_____

What is Isaac Newton remembered as?

_____

_____

What do the Three Laws of Motion tell us?

_____

_____

2.1.6 Observe, sketch, demonstrate, and compare how applied force (push or pull) changes the motion of objects.

Name _____

Essential Question

How Can We Change Motion?

Set a Purpose

Tell what you want to figure out in this investigation.

_____

_____

Think About the Procedure

1 What do you want to do to the cube?

_____

2 List some ideas for how to push the cube.

_____

3 List some ideas for how to pull the cube.

_____

_____

Record Your Data

Draw and write to show what you did.

Action	What I Did
Push	
Pull	

Draw Conclusions

1 How do the string, the straw, and the craft stick change the motion of the cube?

_____

_____

2 How are the push and the pull the same? How are they different?

_____

_____

_____

Ask More Questions

What are some other questions you can ask about changing the motion of a cube?

_____

2.1.7 Investigate the motion of objects when they are acted upon by forces at a distance such as gravity and magnetism.

Lesson 5

Essential Question

What Is Gravity?

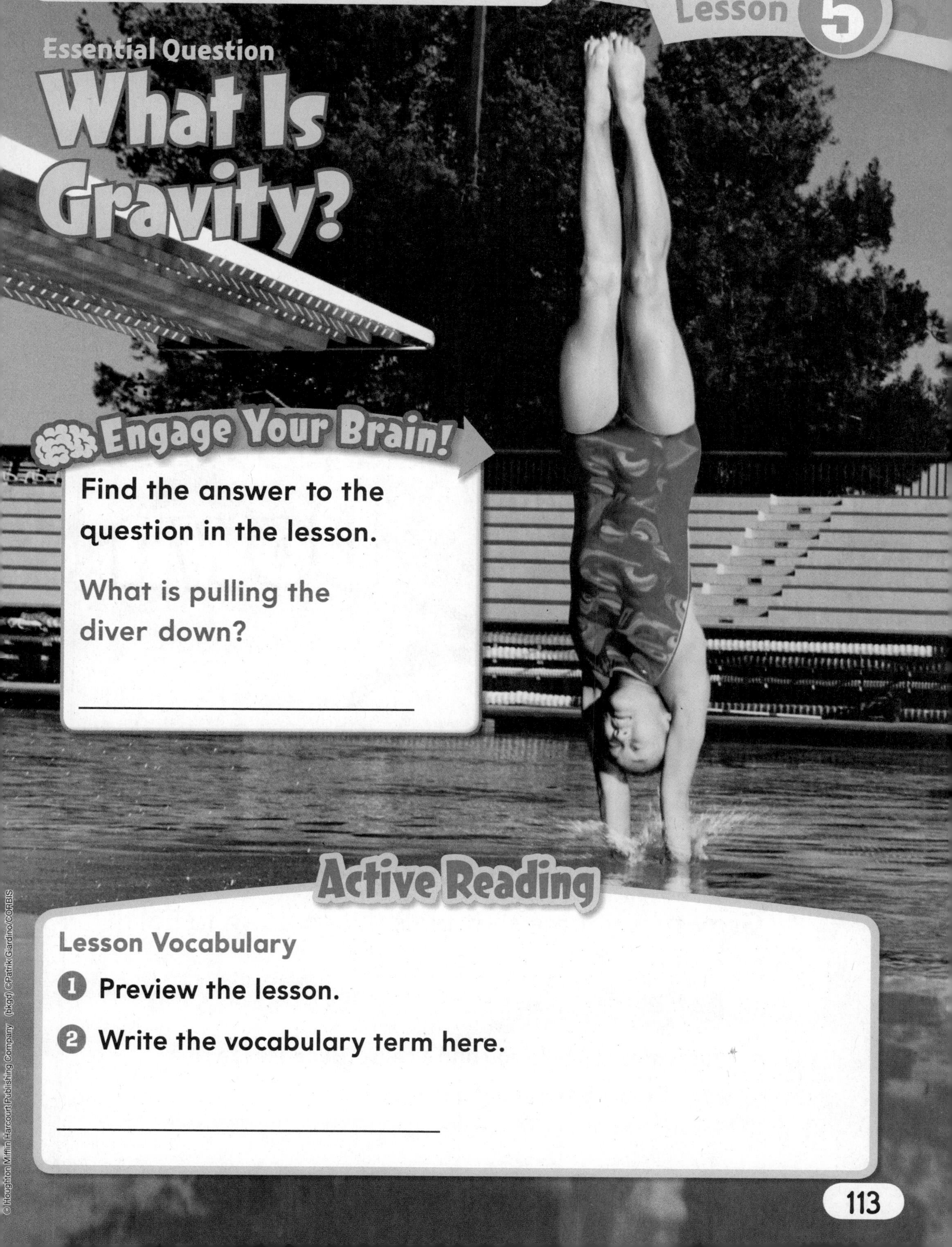

Engage Your Brain!

Find the answer to the question in the lesson.

What is pulling the diver down?

____

Active Reading

Lesson Vocabulary

1. Preview the lesson.
2. Write the vocabulary term here.

____

What Goes Up Must Come Down

Look at the boy jumping. He is up in the air, but soon he will come back down to the ground. Why doesn't he float away? It is because of gravity. **Gravity** is a force that pulls things down to Earth.

Active Reading

Clue words can help you find a cause. **Because** is a clue word. Draw a box around **because**.

Gravity pulls things down unless something holds them up. The bed is holding one girl up off the floor. But when the girl drops the teddy bear, nothing holds it up. Gravity pulls the bear down without touching it.

▶ Where will the teddy bear go? Draw an arrow to show its path.

Sports Fun

Did you know that you use gravity to play sports? You push against gravity every time you move your body or throw something. Pushing against gravity is hard to do. Gravity always pulls things back down to Earth.

The girl pushes against gravity as she throws the ball.

Soon, gravity will pull the ball back down.

The girl pushes against gravity to jump.

► How does the girl use her body to push?

_____

_____

Sum It Up!

1 Think About It!

Look at the first picture. What happens next? Draw to show where the boy goes.

2 Write It!

Look at the boy you drew above. Write two sentences about the pictures. What holds the boy off the ground? What pulls him down the slide?

_____

_____

Name _____

Word Play

Use these words to fill in the blanks.
Then find each word in the puzzle.

gravity	pull	up	down	fall

1. If you drop a ball, it falls _____ .

2. A chair holds you _____ off the ground.

3. You push against _____ when you lift a ball.

4. A book will _____ if nothing holds it up.

5. Gravity can _____ things to Earth.

```
p  u  l  l  r  g  u
b  e  f  e  r  g  p
g  r  a  v  i  t  y
y  e  l  e  d  g  j
o  m  l  t  o  z  v
k  f  u  b  w  w  r
g  n  y  j  n  d  a
```

Apply Concepts

Fill in the web with facts about gravity.

down   Earth   holds   push

Gravity pulls things down to _____ .

You _____ against gravity when you jump.

gravity

An object falls unless something _____ it up.

Gravity pulls objects _____ without touching them.

Take It Home!

Family Members: Have your child name his or her favorite sport and explain how he or she pushes against gravity to play it.

2.1.7 Investigate the motion of objects when they are acted upon by forces at a distance such as gravity and magnetism.

Lesson **6**

Essential Question

What Are Magnets?

Engage Your Brain!

Find the answer to the question in the lesson.

What objects are making this smiley face?

_____

Active Reading

Lesson Vocabulary

1. Preview the lesson.

2. Write the 4 vocabulary terms here.

_____ _____

_____ _____

MAGNETIC PULL

A **magnet** is an object that can pull things made of iron and steel. A magnet can push or pull other magnets.

A magnet has two poles. A **pole** is a place on a magnet where the pull is the greatest. One pole is the north-seeking, or **N**, pole. The other pole is the south-seeking, or **S**, pole.

Active Reading

Find the sentence that tells the meaning of **pole**. Draw a line under the sentence.

bar magnet

horseshoe magnet

ring magnets

Like poles, or poles that are the same, repel each other. **Repel** means to push away from something.

▶ Draw two bar magnets to show another way they can repel.

Opposite poles, or poles that are different, attract each other. **Attract** means to pull toward something.

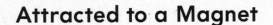

ATTRACT ATTENTION

A steel paper clip is attracted to a magnet. A rubber band is not. Magnets attract some things but not others. Look at these boxes. Which things are attracted to a magnet? Which things are not?

Attracted to a Magnet

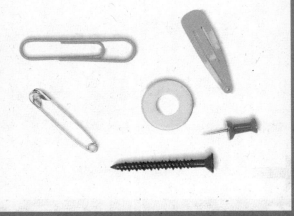

Not Attracted to a Magnet

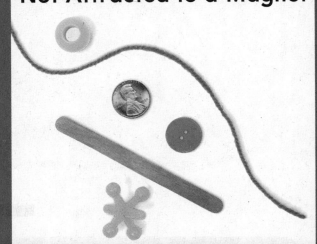

▶ Draw something else that a magnet attracts.

▶ Draw something else that a magnet does not attract.

124

Look at the way the magnet pulls the paper clips right through the hand! A magnet does not have to touch an object to move it. This is possible because of its magnetic field. This is the area around a magnet where the magnetic force is felt.

Do the Math!
Measuring Distance

How far from a paper clip must a magnet be before it does not attract it? Use a ruler to measure.

Distance	Did the magnet attract the paper clip?
½ inch	
1 inch	
1½ inches	
2 inches	

How far from the magnet can you observe the magnetic field? How do you know?

_____

_____

MAGNETS EVERYWHERE

Magnets do much more than stick papers to the refrigerator. They help us in amazing ways! Look at the pictures to see some of the things magnets can do.

Active Reading

A detail is a fact about a main idea. Reread the captions. Draw one line under each of three details about how magnets are used.

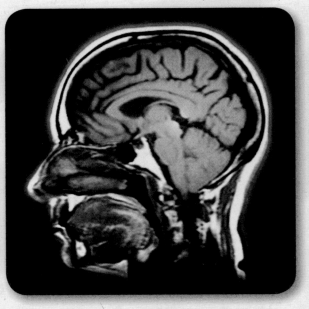

Magnets in MRI machines help make pictures of the inside of our bodies.

Huge magnets help sort items made of iron and steel before they are recycled.

▶ Draw a way you use magnets.

A Maglev train uses magnets to lift and move the train forward. One train has gone 361 miles per hour!

Sum It Up!

1 Circle It!

Circle the objects a magnet attracts.

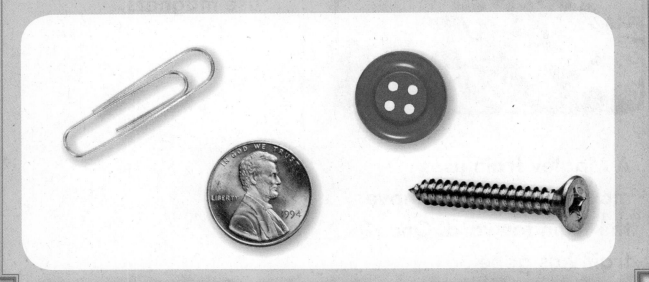

2 Answer It!

Circle true or false to describe the statement.

A magnet must touch an object to attract it.

true   false

3 Draw It!

Draw a way you can use a magnet.

128

Name _____

Word Play

Write a word from the word bank on each line to complete the friendly letter.

magnets	poles	attract	repel

Dear Uncle Herbie,

Thanks for the science kit! I like the _____ the best. They make some objects move without touching them. I used the big magnet to _____ an iron nail.

Each magnet has two places where the pull is the strongest. These places are called _____. When two poles that are the same are pointed toward each other, they _____. They push apart really hard.

Your niece,

Olivia

Apply Concepts

Complete this graphic organizer. Write an important detail about magnets in each box.

Magnets

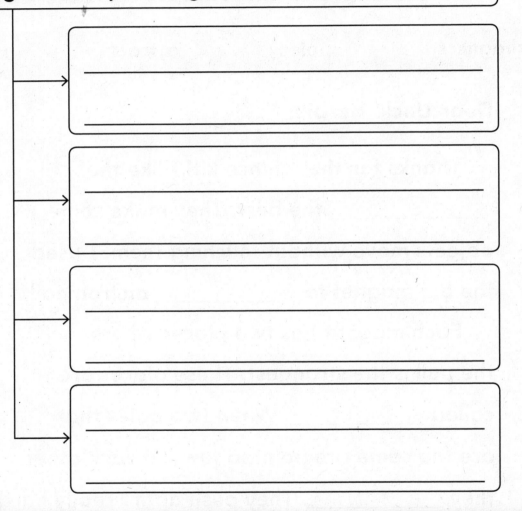

A magnet is an object that can push and pull other magnets and pull things made of iron and steel.

_____

_____

_____

_____

Family Members: Ask your child to tell you about magnets. Ask him or her to point out how magnets work and how they are used in everyday life.

© Houghton Mifflin Harcourt Publishing Company

Review and ISTEP+ Practice

Name _____

Multiple Choice
Fill in the circle next to the best answer.

2.1.6
1 What is speed?
- ○ how fast something moves
- ○ the way something changes
- ○ where something is

2.1.4
2 Which do you move round and round on?
- ○ a carousel
- ○ a slide
- ○ a swing

2.1.6
3 Which is a force?
- ○ looking at the sky
- ○ pushing a bike
- ○ reading a book

2.1.4
4 The black ball is hanging from a string. You pull the ball back and let it go. What kind of motion does the ball make?
- ○ back and forth
- ○ round and round
- ○ straight line

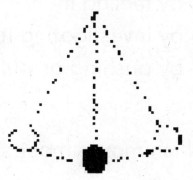

2.1.4

5 What question does the picture answer?

○ How can a ball move?

○ Who wins the game?

○ Is the ball filled with air?

2.1.6

6 How do you change the motion of an object?

○ by feeling it

○ by investigating it

○ by pushing or pulling it

2.1.4

7 Which moves most slowly?

○ a bike

○ a car

○ a train

2.1.4

8 How are these ducks moving?

○ in a circle

○ in a straight line

○ in a zigzag

2.1.4

9 Which word tells about how fast a train moves?

○ motion

○ speed

○ straight

2.1.6

10 Which picture shows a force?

○

○

○

2.1.5

11 What tells where an object is located?

○ direction

○ position

○ speed

2.1.6

12 What happens when this boy pushes the swing?

○ The swing changes direction.

○ The swing stops moving.

○ The swing moves toward the boy.

2.1.5

13 How has the dog changed position?

- ◯ It has moved out of the box.
- ◯ It has moved into the box.
- ◯ It is now behind the box.

2.1.5

14 Where is the girl?

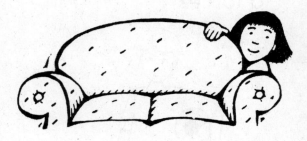

- ◯ in front of the couch
- ◯ on the couch
- ◯ behind the couch

2.1.7

15 What does gravity do?
- ◯ It lifts things away from Earth.
- ◯ It pulls things toward Earth.
- ◯ It pushes things away from you.

2.1.7

16 Which shows how gravity works?

○ A balloon floats in the air.

○ A plane flies overhead.

○ An apple falls to the ground.

2.1.7

17 Gravity pulls on the books. What keeps the books from falling?

○ The books are too light.

○ The desk holds them up.

○ The stack of books is too big.

2.1.7

18 Which object does a magnet attract?

○ a sheet of paper

○ a steel paper clip

○ a wood pencil

2.1.7

19 You hold up these magnets.

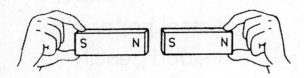

How do you know they will attract each other?

○ Opposite poles attract each other.

○ They are the same size.

○ Like poles attract each other.

2.1.7

20 What does this picture show?

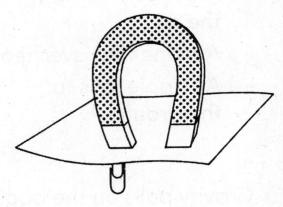

○ how a piece of paper attracts a paper clip

○ how a magnet can move an object without touching it

○ how a magnet repels a steel paper clip

Weather and the Sky

a tornado in Indiana

I Wonder Why

People keep extra food and other supplies in case of a storm. Why?
Turn the page to find out.

Here's Why People keep extra supplies in case the power goes out and the stores are closed.

Track Your Progress

Essential Questions and Indiana Standards

STANDARD 2 Earth Science

Day to day and over the seasons observe, measure, record, recognize patterns and ask questions about features of weather.

STANDARD 2 Earth Science

Investigate how the position of the sun and moon and the shape of the moon change in observable patterns.

© Houghton Mifflin Harcourt Publishing Company (bkgd) ©Getty Images Royalty Free; (t) © Roy Morsch/Corbis; (b) ©Kathy Collins/Getty (Careers) ©Erik Nguyen/Corbis; (5) ©Tim Sloan/Getty (Careers) ©Erik Nguyen/Getty Images (border) ©NHbo/Age Fotostock

2.2.1 Construct and use tools to observe and measure weather phenomena such as precipitation, changes in temperature, wind speed and direction. **2.2.2** Experience and describe wind (moving air) as motion of the air that surrounds us and takes up space. **2.2.3** Chart or graph weather observations such as cloud cover, cloud type, and type of precipitation on a daily basis over a period of weeks.

Essential Question

How Does Weather Change?

Engage Your Brain!

Find the answer to the question in the lesson.

What kind of weather do these clouds bring?

_____

Active Reading

Lesson Vocabulary

① Preview the lesson.

② Write the 4 vocabulary terms here.

_____   _____

_____   _____

Wonderful Weather

Weather is what the air outside is like. Weather may be sunny, rainy, cloudy, snowy, or windy. It can be hot or cold outside. Weather can change quickly, or it can change over many days or months.

Active Reading

The main idea is the most important idea about something. Draw a line under the main idea on this page.

Some days are warm and sunny.

▶ Draw what the weather is like today.

On some days, rain falls.

In some places, the weather gets very cold. Snow may fall.

141

Send In the Clouds

A cloud is a group of tiny drops of water or ice crystals. The drops are so light that they float in the air. The water drops may get bigger and heavier. When the drops get too heavy to float, they fall as rain or snow.

Clouds are clues about how the weather may change.

Active Reading

An effect tells what happens. Draw a line under the effect of the water drops getting too heavy to float.

Cumulus clouds are white and puffy. They usually mean sunny weather.

Stratus clouds are gray and flat. They often cover the sky. Stratus clouds may bring rain or snow.

▶ Draw clouds that bring rain. Label your picture.

Cirrus clouds are high in the sky. These thin, wispy clouds usually mean sunny weather.

Cumulonimbus clouds are thunderstorm clouds. These clouds are tall and puffy.

143

Measure It!

You can use tools to measure weather.
A rain gauge measures precipitation.
Precipitation is water that falls from the sky.
Rain, snow, sleet, and hail are precipitation.
A thermometer measures temperature.
Temperature is how hot or cold something is.

Active Reading

Find the sentence that tells the meaning of **precipitation**. Draw a line under it.

Air is all around us. **Wind** is moving air that surrounds us and takes up space. A weather vane tells the direction of the wind.

This thermometer measures temperature in degrees Fahrenheit and Celsius.

A rain gauge tells how much rain falls.

Do the Math!

Measure Temperature

Use a thermometer to measure the temperature of the air in the morning and in the afternoon. Color the pictures below to show the temperatures. Write the temperatures on the lines.

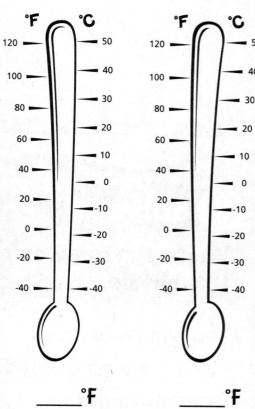

Morning

Afternoon

_____°F   _____°F

Write a subtraction sentence to find out how the temperature changed.

_____

Sum It Up!

① Draw It!

Draw your favorite kind of weather.

② Match It!

Match each tool to what it measures.

temperature

rain

③ Solve It!

Write the answer to this riddle.

You can't see me,
  but I am all around.
I am moving air.
I take up space.
  What am I?

_____

④ Order It!

Write 1, 2, 3 to order these thermometers from hottest to coldest. Use 1 for the hottest.

_____   _____   _____

Name _____

Word Play

Read the clues. Use the words to complete the puzzle.

weather   temperature   precipitation   wind

Across

① What the air outside is like

② Moving air that surrounds you and takes up space

Down

③ Water that falls as rain, snow, sleet, or hail

④ How hot or cold something is

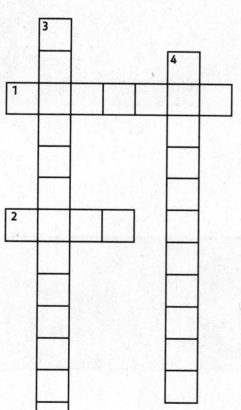

Apply Concepts

Write and draw to complete the chart.

Cloud and Weather

Cloud	Weather
	Cumulus clouds mean sunny weather.
	_____ _____
	Cirrus clouds bring sunny weather.
	_____ _____

© Houghton Mifflin Harcourt Publishing Company   (tl) ©Corbis; (bl) ©David R. Frazier/Photo Researchers, Inc.

Take It Home!

Family Members: Observe clouds with your child for a week. Ask your child to use clues from the clouds to predict the weather each day.

2.2.1 Construct and use tools to observe and measure weather phenomena such as precipitation, changes in temperature, wind speed and direction.

Name _____

Essential Question

How Can We Measure Precipitation?

Set a Purpose

Tell what you want to find out.

_____

Think About the Procedure

1 Why do you make marks on the bottle?

_____

_____

2 Why do you measure each day for two weeks?

_____

_____

_____

Record Your Data

In each box, write the day's precipitation in inches and **R** for rain, **SN** for snow, **SL** for sleet, and **H** for hail.

	Day 1	Day 2	Day 3	Day 4	Day 5	Day 6	Day 7
Week 1							
Week 2							

Draw Conclusions

On which day did the most precipitation fall? How do you know?

_____

_____

Did you observe any weather patterns? Explain.

_____

_____

Ask More Questions

What other questions could you ask about measuring weather?

_____

_____

150

2.2.4 Ask questions about charted observations and graphed data. Identify the patterns and cycles of weather day-to-day as well as seasonal time scales in terms of temperature and rainfall/snowfall amounts. **2.2.7** Investigate how the sun appears to move through the sky during the day by observing and drawing the length and direction of shadows.

Essential Question

What Are Some Weather Patterns?

Engage Your Brain!

Find the answer to the question in the lesson.

When might you see ice on plants?

You might see this in _____.

Active Reading

Lesson Vocabulary

1 Preview the lesson.

2 Write the 5 vocabulary terms here.

_____   _____

_____   _____

_____

A Perfect Pattern

Weather can change from hour to hour and from day to day. It changes in a pattern. A **weather pattern** is a weather change that repeats over and over.

Gentle Morning

The sun is low in the sky. It is just starting to warm Earth. The air is still cool.

Afternoon So Bright

The sun is high in the sky. It has warmed Earth and the air.

Houghton Mifflin Harcourt Publishing Company

▶ Which part of the day is warmest?

_____

Evening Shade

The sun is setting. It no longer warms Earth as much. The air is cooling.

Night Fall

We can not see the sun. The air is cooler. Tomorrow the pattern will begin again.

153

Where Does the Water Go?

The **water cycle** is the way water moves from Earth's surface into the air and back again. The water cycle is another pattern. The water cycle causes weather to change.

The sun's heat makes water **evaporate**, or change to a gas. The gas is pushed up and meets cooler air.

▶ Where will the water go when the sun heats it?

_____

_____

_____

Then the gas cools and condenses, or changes into tiny drops of water. The drops form clouds.

© Houghton Mifflin Harcourt Publishing Company

Active Reading

A cause tells why something happens. What causes water drops to fall as rain or snow? Draw one line under the cause.

The water drops join to make bigger ones. The drops fall as precipitation.

The precipitation flows into rivers, lakes, and oceans. Then the water cycle starts again.

Season to Season

A **season** is a time of year that has a certain kind of weather. Weather changes each season. The seasons follow the same pattern every year.

▶ Draw winter clothes on the boy.

Fabulous Fall

In fall the air outside may be cool. The leaves of some trees change color and drop off.

Wonderful Winter

Winter is the coldest season. In some places snow may fall. The sun looks low in the sky. Shadows are longer.

▶ Draw an activity you do during summer.

Sunny Spring

In spring the air gets warmer. Some places get a lot of rain.

Super Summer

Summer is the warmest season. Some places have sudden storms. The sun looks high in the sky. Shadows are shorter.

Sum It Up!

① Draw It!

Draw yourself outside in your favorite season.

② Match It!

Match each picture to the word that tells about it.

morning

afternoon

③ Answer It!

Fill in the blank.

What is the movement of water from Earth's surface into the air and back again called?

_____

④ Order It!

Number the seasons to show their order. Start with winter.

___1___ winter

_____ summer

_____ fall

_____ spring

Name _____

Word Play

Fill in the blanks with words from the box.

| season | evaporate | condense | water |

$\frac{}{1}$ _ _ _ _ moves in a cycle.

Heat can cause water to change to a gas, or

_ _ $\frac{}{2}$ _ _ _ _ $\frac{}{3}$ _ .

Winter is a _ _ $\frac{}{4}$ _ _ _ .

Water can _ _ _ _ $\frac{}{5}$ $\frac{}{6}$ _ _ into drops.

Use the circled letters to write the answer to the question.

What do you call a weather change that repeats over and over?

a $\frac{}{1}$ e $\frac{}{2}$ $\frac{}{3}$ her p $\frac{}{4}$ t t $\frac{}{5}$ r $\frac{}{6}$

Apply Concepts

Fill in the chart. Show causes and effects in the water cycle.

Water Cycle

Cause | **Effect**

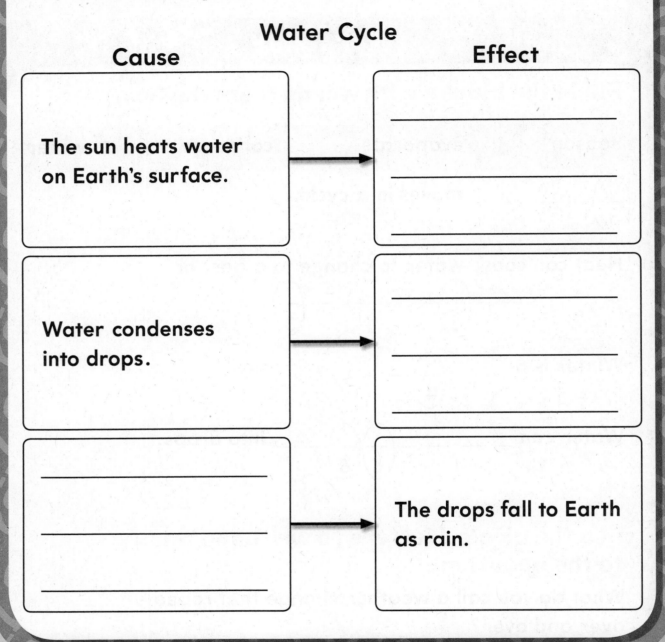

The sun heats water on Earth's surface. →

_____

_____

_____

Water condenses into drops. →

_____

_____

_____

_____

→ The drops fall to Earth as rain.

Take It Home!

Family Members: Watch or read a daily weather forecast with your child. Talk about why it can be helpful to predict weather.

 **Inquiry Flipchart p. 21**

Lesson 4
INQUIRY

 2.2.5 Ask questions and design class investigations on the effect of the sun heating the surface of the earth.

Name _____

Essential Question

How Does the Sun Heat Earth?

Set a Purpose

Write what you want to find out.

_____

_____

State Your Hypothesis

Write your hypothesis, or the statement that you will test.

_____

_____

Think About the Procedure

How will you use the thermometers?

_____

_____

Record Your Data

In this chart, record what you observe.

	Starting Temperature	Ending Temperature
air		
water		
soil		

Draw Conclusions

How does the sun heat Earth's land, air, and water differently?
How do you know?

_____

_____

_____

Ask More Questions

What other questions can you ask about the sun's heat?

_____

_____

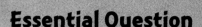

Essential Question

How Can We Prepare for Severe Weather?

Engage Your Brain!

Find the answer to the question in the lesson.

When can wind take the shape of a cone?

when there is a

_____

Active Reading

Lesson Vocabulary

❶ Preview the lesson.

❷ Write the 4 vocabulary terms here.

_____   _____

_____   _____

Wild Weather

Sometimes weather gets wild! Then we have severe, or very bad, weather. A thunderstorm is one kind of severe weather. A **thunderstorm** is a storm with a lot of rain, thunder, and lightning.

Active Reading

A detail is a fact about a main idea. Draw one line under a detail. Draw an arrow to the main idea it tells about.

Lightning is a flash of electricity in the sky.

A tornado is a kind of severe weather, too. A **tornado** is a spinning cloud with a cone shape. A tornado has very strong winds.

Another kind of severe weather is a hurricane. A **hurricane** is a large storm with heavy rain and strong winds.

▶ What weather does this picture show? Label it.

_____

A hurricane can cause a lot of damage to an area.

Safety First

Storms can be dangerous. Scientists called meteorologists predict storms. They warn people about storms. Then people can do things to stay safe and be prepared for storms.

Meteorologists use tools such as computers to help predict and track severe weather.

▶ What might happen if meteorologists couldn't predict weather in your area?

_____

_____

Tips for Storm Safety

Read these tips on how to get ready for a storm. Then add your own tip at the bottom.

1. Get extra food and water.

2. Get other things you may need, such as flashlights and blankets.

3. Make a plan for your family and pets.

4. Stay inside.

5. _____

   _____

   _____

People try to protect property from severe weather.

Sum It Up!

① Solve It!

Fill in the blank.

What kind of storm

is made up of

and  ?

_____

② Draw It!

Draw yourself preparing for severe weather.

③ Circle It!

Circle the pictures that show severe weather.

Brain Check

Name _____

Word Play

Find each word in the puzzle. Then answer the questions.

| thunderstorm | hurricane | lightning | tornado |

```
q i g g d o r a s t i e
t h u n d e r s t o r m
l s j k d a z y l r p a
e v h u r r i c a n e m
w a t r s p l i t a r f
b w e g l n o w t d u i
l i g h t n i n g o r b
```

1. What might you see during a thunderstorm?

_____

2. What kind of storm always has heavy rain and strong winds?

_____

169

Apply Concepts

How would you prepare for severe weather in your area? Write a plan.

_____

_____

_____

_____

_____

_____

_____

_____

_____

Family Members: Work with your child to make a storm safety plan for your family.

Ask a Storm Chaser

What kinds of storms do storm chasers look for?
Most storm chasers look for tornadoes. A few storm chasers look for hurricanes.

How do you work?
Storm chasers watch the weather carefully. We learn about bad storms. We try to predict where to find them. Then we drive to see a storm.

How does storm chasing help other people?
Most storm chasers work with weather centers. If we spot a storm, we can alert the police and people on farms.

Now It's Your Turn!

▶ What question would you ask a storm chaser?

_____

_____

Safety from the Storm

▶ Draw or write the answer to each question to get to safety.

1 Your family has a storm kit. You use it if you lose power or get hurt. Draw one thing you would put in a storm kit.

2 A storm might be coming. Why should you make a plan?

3 Storm chasers spot a tornado. Draw a picture of what they might see.

4 Tornado warning! Your family follows its safety plan by finding shelter. Why?

1

2

3

4

2.2.7 Investigate how the sun appears to move through the sky during the day by observing and drawing the length and direction of shadows. **2.2.8** Investigate how the moon appears to move through the sky during the day by observing and drawing its location at different times. **2.2.9** Investigate how the shape of the moon changes from day to day in a repeating cycle that lasts about a month.

Lesson **6**

Essential Question

How Do the Sun and Moon Seem to Change?

Engage Your Brain!

Find the answer to the question in the lesson.

When can you see the moon?

at _____ and sometimes in the _____

Active Reading

Lesson Vocabulary

1. Preview the lesson.
2. Write the 4 vocabulary terms here.

_____   _____

_____   _____

Hello Sunshine

sun

You can see many things in the daytime sky. You may see clouds or even the moon. But the brightest thing in the daytime sky is the sun.

The **sun** is the star closest to Earth. A **star** is an object in the sky that gives off its own light. The sun lights and heats Earth.

Active Reading

The main idea is the most important idea about something. Draw two lines under the main idea.

morning

Each day the sun seems to move across the sky. Its light makes shadows. As the position of the sun changes, shadows change, too. The sun's light shines on objects from different directions as the day goes on.

▶ Look at the shadows in the pictures. Draw an arrow on each picture to show where the sunlight is coming from.

noon

afternoon

Good night Moon

Now it is night. You may see stars, planets, and the moon. The **moon** is a huge ball of rock that does not give off its own light. The moon reflects light from the sun.

Active Reading

Find the sentence that tells the meaning of **moon**. Draw a line under the sentence.

first quarter moon, day 8

new moon, day 1

The moon moves across the sky. The moon's shape seems to change, too. The **phases**, or shapes you see, change as the moon moves. The changes follow a repeating pattern that lasts about a month.

▶ Look in the sky at night. Draw what you see.

full moon, day 15

third quarter moon, day 22

Sum It Up!

① Draw it!

Draw the boy's shadow at different times of day.

morning

noon

② Order It!

Number the moon phases to show their order. Start with the new moon.

1 _____

_____

_____

_____

178

Brain Check

Lesson **6**

Name _____

Word Play

Unscramble the letters. Then write the word to complete each sentence.

sshpae   You can observe the __ __ __ __ __ __ of the moon. Look at how the moon seems to change its shape.

omon   The __ __ __ __ is a huge ball of rock that does not give off its own light.

shdwsao   As the position of the sun seems to change, __ __ __ __ __ __ __ change too.

usn   The closest star to Earth is the __ __ __ .

rast   A __ __ __ __ is an object in the sky that gives off its own light.

© Houghton Mifflin Harcourt Publishing Company

Apply Concepts

Fill in the diagram to compare the sun and the moon.

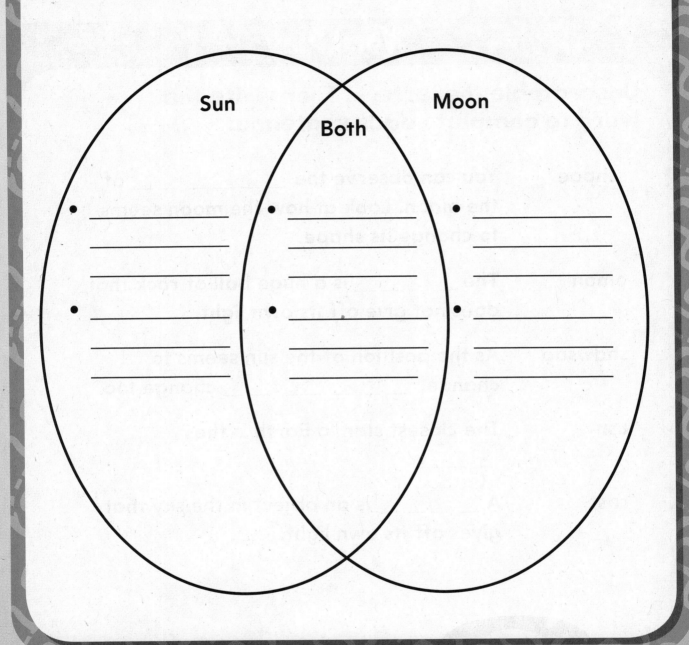

Sun

Both

Moon

Take It Home!

Family Members: Look at the sky with your child for a few nights in a row. Observe the moon. Ask your child to describe how the moon moves and seems to change shape.

Multiple Choice

Fill in the circle next to the best answer.

2.2.5

1 Which does the sun warm the most in one hour?

○ air

○ soil

○ water

2.2.2

2 Which picture shows wind?

○

○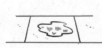

○

○

2.2.1, 2.2.4

3 You measure the temperature at 10 in the morning during the week.

Monday	60 °F
Tuesday	68 °F
Wednesday	64 °F

Which is TRUE?

○ Monday was hotter than Tuesday.

○ Tuesday was hotter than Monday.

○ Wednesday was hotter than Tuesday.

2.2.4

4 Which is TRUE of winter and spring?

○ Spring is usually colder than winter.

○ Winter is usually colder than spring.

○ Winter and spring usually have about the same temperatures.

2.2.6

5 Why should people listen to meteorologists to keep safe from severe weather?

○ Meteorologists name storms.

○ Meteorologists stop severe weather.

○ Meteorologists warn people about severe weather.

2.2.1, 2.2.2

6 What do you measure with this tool?

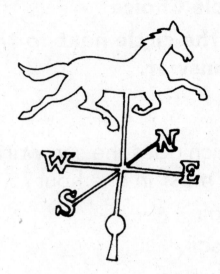

○ the direction of the wind

○ rainfall

○ temperature

2.2.3

7 You observe the weather for five days and make this chart.

Monday	mostly cloudy
Tuesday	sunny
Wednesday	partly cloudy
Thursday	mostly cloudy
Friday	sunny

Which conclusion is TRUE?

○ It was sunny more days than it was cloudy.

○ It was cloudy more days than it was sunny.

○ The weather stayed the same during the week.

2.2.1, 2.2.3

8 You want to observe and measure out how much it rains each day for two weeks. Which tool would you make and use?

○ a rain gauge

○ a thermometer

○ a weather vane

2.2.3

9 It rained all day yesterday. What type of cloud did you MOST LIKELY see?

○ cirrus

○ cumulus

○ stratus

Use this chart to answer questions 10 and 11.

Month	Average Temperature	Total Rainfall
January	26 °F	2.5 in.
April	52 °F	3.6 in.
July	75 °F	4.4 in.
October	54 °F	2.7 in.

2.2.4

10 In which two months was the average temperature about the SAME?

○ January and July

○ July and October

○ April and October

2.2.4

11 When did it rain the MOST?

○ April

○ July

○ October

Nature of Science, 2.2.5

12 Abram is doing an experiment with the materials shown here.

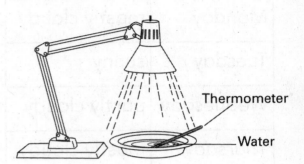

Thermometer

Water

What is he trying to find out?

○ how the sun heats water

○ how wind moves water

○ how water can move

2.2.6

13 Which kind of severe weather does this picture show?

○ a blizzard
○ a hurricane
○ a tornado

2.2.6

14 What should you do during a tornado?

○ run outside
○ stand under a tree
○ stay inside a safe place

2.2.7

15 Which is TRUE?

○ As the position of the sun seems to change, shadows change, too.
○ Shadows are always in front of objects.
○ Shadows are always the same size.

2.2.7

16 What time of day is shown in this picture?

○ noon
○ afternoon
○ night

2.2.8

17 Which is TRUE?

○ The moon appears to move across the sky.

○ The moon shines light onto Earth.

○ The motion of the moon changes once a month.

2.2.9

18 In which phase do we see MOST of the moon?

○ first quarter moon

○ full moon

○ third quarter moon

2.2.9

19 Which phase of the moon does this picture show?

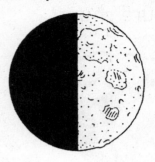

○ first quarter moon

○ full moon

○ new moon

2.2.9

20 This is the moon you saw in the sky last night.

Which moon would you see in about one month?

○ first quarter moon

○ full moon

○ new moon

a box turtle
in Indiana

I Wonder Why

Mother box turtles bury their
eggs. Why?
Turn the page to find out.

Here's Why Mother box turtles need to keep their eggs warm and safe for the young turtles to hatch.

Track Your Progress

Essential Questions and Indiana Standards

STANDARD 3
Life Science

Observe, ask questions about, and describe how organisms change their forms and behavior in the course of their life cycles.

2.3.1 Observing closely over a period of time, record in pictures and words the changes in plants and animals throughout their life cycles, including details of their body plan, structure and timing of growth, reproduction and death. **2.3.2** Compare and contrast details of body plan and structure within the life cycles of plants and animals.

Essential Question

What Are Some Animal Life Cycles?

 Engage Your Brain!

Find the answer to the riddle in this lesson.

When is a frog not like a frog?

when it is a

_____

 Active Reading

Lesson Vocabulary

1. Preview the lesson.

2. Write the 6 vocabulary terms here.

_____   _____

_____   _____

_____   _____

Animal Start-Ups

A dog can have puppies. A cat can have kittens. Adult animals can **reproduce**, or have young. Animals such as puppies and kittens look like their parents. How does a kitten look like an adult cat?

Other young animals look very different from their parents. They go through changes and become like their parents.

A young butterfly does not look like its parents.

A young cat looks like its parents.

▶ **Name another animal that looks like its parents.**

_____

Animals change as they grow. The changes that happen to an animal during its life make up its **life cycle**.

During its lifetime, an animal is born or hatches. It grows and changes, reproduces, and dies.

▶ How are the animals in this chart alike?

_____

_____

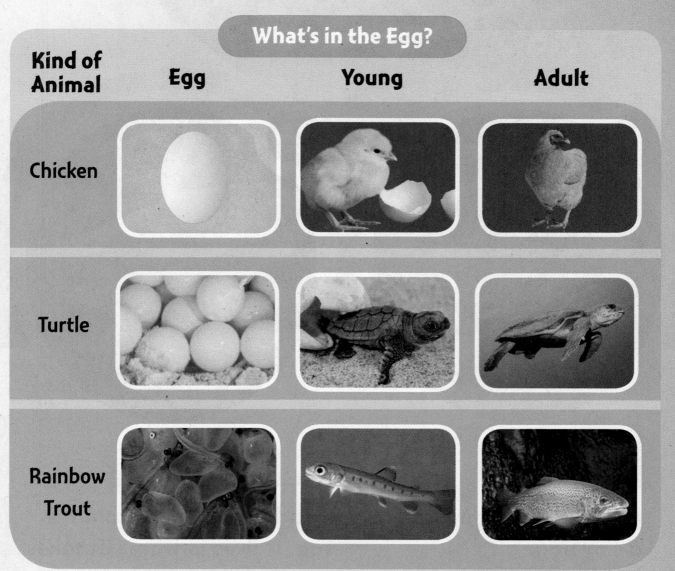

What's in the Egg?

Kind of Animal	Egg	Young	Adult
Chicken			
Turtle			
Rainbow Trout			

Egg

A frog begins life inside a tiny egg.

Young Tadpole

A tadpole hatches from the egg. It lives in water. It takes in oxygen with gills.

Hatch, Swim, Hop

Did you know that a frog begins life inside a tiny egg? The young frog goes through changes to become an adult. These changes are called **metamorphosis**.

Active Reading

Circle the name of the body parts that a tadpole uses to take in oxygen. Underline the name of the body parts that an adult frog uses to take in oxygen.

Growing Tadpole

The tadpole gets bigger. It grows four legs. Later, it loses its tail.

Frog

The adult frog lives on land or in water until it dies. It hops. It breathes with lungs.

Polar Parenting

It is late October. A female polar bear gets a shelter ready for her cubs. She digs a den in the snow. The den will keep her young warm and safe. She gives birth in winter.

> ▶ How is a polar bear's life cycle different from a frog's life cycle?
>
> _____

Newborn

A polar bear cub is born inside the den. It drinks milk from its mother's body.

Growing Cub

The cub begins to explore outside the den.

© Houghton Mifflin Harcourt Publishing Company (bkgd) ©Steve Bloom Images/Alamy; (cr) ©All Canada Photos/Alamy; (cl) ©Jenny E. Ross/Corbis;

We'll stay with our mother for almost three years, until we're grown up.

3

4

Young Polar Bear

The young polar bear learns to swim and hunt.

Adult Polar Bear

The adult polar bear lives on its own until its death.

The Mighty Monarch

A monarch butterfly has a life cycle, too. An adult female butterfly lays a tiny egg. The egg is so small it is hard to see. This picture shows a close-up of an egg on a leaf.

1 egg

▶ Why do you think a butterfly egg is so small?

_____

_____

2 larva

A tiny **larva**, or caterpillar, hatches from the egg. A caterpillar is a young butterfly. The larva eats a lot and grows quickly.

Then, the larva stops eating and moving. The larva becomes a pupa. It makes a hard covering.

A **pupa** goes through metamorphosis inside the covering. It grows wings. Many other changes also happen.

3 pupa

4 adult

Finally, an adult butterfly comes out of the covering. It can have its own young.

Active Reading

Clue words can help you find the order of events. Draw boxes around the clue words **then** and **finally**.

Sum It Up!

① Mark It!

Mark an X on the animal that does not look like its young.

② Draw It!

Draw a picture of this animal's mother.

③ Solve It!

Answer the riddle.

I am little now.
I will change and grow.
Someday I will be an adult cat.
What am I? _____

④ Think About It!

Is a 👶 most like a 🐻 , a 🦎 , or a 🐛 ? Why?

Name _____

Word Play

Use these words to complete the puzzle.

tadpole   change   pupa   larva   reproduce   cycle

Across

1. The stage in a butterfly's life cycle after the egg

2. To make more living things of the same kind

Down

3. The stage in a butterfly's life between larva and adult

4. A young frog that lives in water

5. This takes place during metamorphosis in frogs and butterflies.

6. The changes in an animal's life from when it starts life until it dies is its life _____

How is the life cycle of a butterfly different from the life cycle of a polar bear? Use this chart to show your answer.

Life Cycles

Butterfly	Polar Bear
A butterfly hatches from an egg.	_____ _____
_____ _____	A polar bear cub drinks milk from its mother's body.
_____ _____	A polar bear cub looks a lot like its parents.
A butterfly larva does not stay with its parents.	_____ _____

Take It Home!

Family Members: Discuss life cycles with your child. Sort family photographs to show ways that your child and others have grown and changed over the years.

2.3.1 Observing closely over a period of time, record in pictures and words the changes in plants and animals throughout their life cycles, including details of their body plan, structure and timing of growth, reproduction and death.

People in **Science**

Learn About ...
Salim Ali

Salim Ali is called the "Birdman of India." He traveled around India to study birds in their habitats. Ali discovered some kinds of birds. He wrote books about the birds he observed. Many people enjoyed reading his books.

Fun Fact

Bird watchers use binoculars like these to see birds more closely.

201

Watch the Bird Grow!

Salim Ali learned about birds. You can learn about birds, too.

▶ Order the life cycle of a robin. Number the pictures from 1 to 4.

young robin

adult robin

robin chick

robin eggs

▶ How is a robin's life cycle like the life cycles of other animals you know?

_____

_____

_____

_____

_____

_____

2.3.2 Compare and contrast details of body plan and structure within the life cycles of plants and animals.

Name _____

Essential Question

How Does a Bean Plant Grow?

Set a Purpose

Explain what you will learn from this activity.

_____

_____

Think About the Procedure

1 Why must you give the plant water and sunlight?

_____

_____

2 Compare the way that your bean plant grew with the way that a classmate's bean plant grew. What was the same?

_____

_____

_____

Record Your Data

In this chart, record what you observe.

Date	Observations

Draw Conclusions

How did the bean plant change?

_____

_____

_____

Ask More Questions

What other questions could you ask about how plants grow?

_____

_____

2.3.1 Observing closely over a period of time, record in pictures and words the changes in plants and animals throughout their life cycles, including details of their body plan, structure and timing of growth, reproduction and death. **2.3.2** Compare and contrast details of body plan and structure within the life cycles of plants and animals.

Essential Question

What Are Some Plant Life Cycles?

Engage Your Brain!

Find the answer to the question in this lesson.

What does the flower part of a dandelion make?

It makes

_____ .

Active Reading

Lesson Vocabulary

1 Preview the lesson.

2 Write the 4 vocabulary terms here.

_____   _____

_____   _____

Plant Start-Ups

Plants are living things. They grow and change. They have life cycles. Most plant life cycles begin with a **seed**. New plants grow from seeds. The growing plants start to look like their parent plants.

Active Reading

Find the words that tell about seeds. Draw a line under the words.

The plants in this garden grew from seeds.

How Fast Do Plants Grow?

Some plants grow quickly. Plants in a vegetable garden take just a few months to become adult plants. Other plants, such as trees, take many years to become adults.

Do the Math!
Interpret a Table

Use the chart to answer the question.

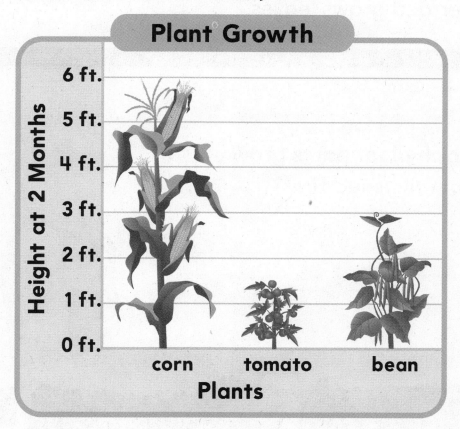

Plant Growth

▶ How much taller did the corn plant grow than the bean plant?

Start with a Seed

What happens when you plant a seed? When a seed gets warmth, air, and water, it may germinate. **Germinate** means to start to grow. The stem of the tiny plant breaks through the ground. The plant gets taller and grows leaves.

▶ Which plant parts grow from the seed first?

_____

A tiny plant is inside a seed.

The seed germinates. The roots grow down.

The stem grows up toward the light.

Growing Up

The tiny plant inside the seed has become a young plant called a **seedling**.

The seedling grows into an adult plant. An adult plant can make flowers and seeds.

Active Reading

Find the words that tell the meaning of **seedling**. Draw a line under those words.

The plant grows more roots and leaves.

The adult plant grows flowers.

Apples
All Around

Some plants have flowers that make seeds and fruit. Parts of the flower grow into fruit. The fruit grows around the seeds to hold and protect them.

Active Reading

Circle the word **seeds** each time you see it on these two pages.

apple blossoms

Parts of apple blossoms grow into apples. The apples grow around seeds.

A Long Life

Some plants have short lives. They die soon after their flowers make seeds. Other plants, such as apple trees, can live for many years. An apple tree can live for a hundred years or more!

adult apple tree

▶ **What do apple blossoms make?**

Inside a Cone

Some plants, like pine trees, do not have flowers. But they do have seeds. Where do their seeds grow? A **cone** is a part of a pine tree and some other plants. Seeds grow inside the cone.

closed pinecones

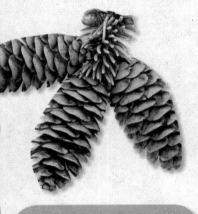

open pinecones with seeds

The cone protects the seeds until they are ready to germinate. Then the cone opens up, and the seeds can fall out.

▶ Where do pine seeds form?

Pine Tree Beginnings

Pine seeds fall to the ground and germinate. As the seedlings grow, they start to look like their parent plants. After a few years, the pine trees grow cones and make seeds. The life cycle begins again.

adult pine trees

▶ What happens after an adult pine tree grows cones and makes seeds?

_____

_____

Sum It Up!

1 Draw It!

Draw the missing step in the plant's life cycle.
Label your picture.

seed   _____   seedling   adult

2 Mark It!

Draw an X on the plant part that does not have seeds.

3 Think About It!

How are flowers and pinecones alike?

_____

_____

Name _____

Word Play

Read each word. Trace a path through the maze to connect each word to its picture.

seed   cone   flower   seedling

Write to tell about the life cycle of a plant. Use the words <u>germinate</u>, <u>seed</u>, and <u>seedling</u>.

Life Cycle of a Plant

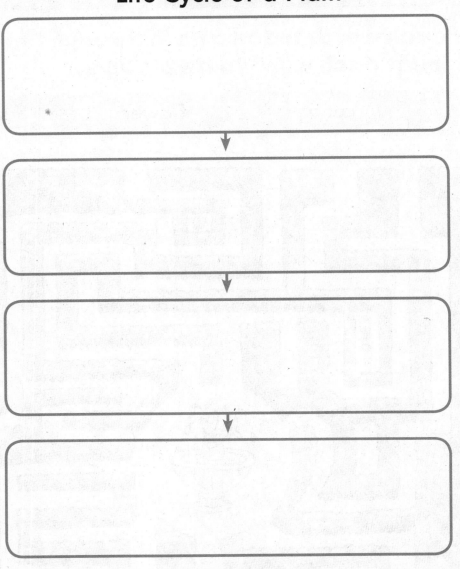

Take It Home!

Family Members: Ask your child to tell you about plant life cycles. Then take a walk around your neighborhood. Talk about the plants you see.

Review and ISTEP+ Practice

Multiple Choice

Fill in the circle next to the best answer.

2.3.1, 2.3.2

1 Which animal hatches from an egg?

○

○

○

2.3.1, 2.3.2

2 During which stage of a butterfly's life cycle does the butterfly make a hard covering?

○ egg

○ larva

○ pupa

2.3.2

3 How are the life cycles of an apple tree and a pine tree the SAME?

○ They both have flowers that grow into fruits.

○ They both have cones that hold seeds.

○ They both make seeds.

2.3.1, 2.3.2

4 Which shows the correct order of the life cycle of a bean plant?

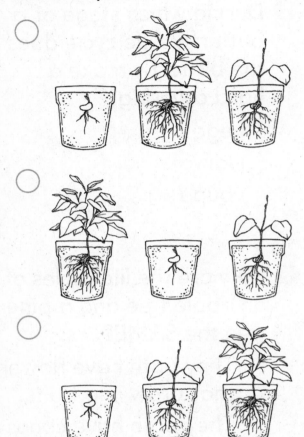

○

○

○

2.3.1, 2.3.2

5 Gabriel is looking at this plant in his backyard.

He knows it is an adult plant. How does he know?
○ The plant has leaves.
○ The plant has a flower.
○ The plant is dead.

2.3.1, 2.3.2

6 What helps a tadpole take in oxygen?
○ gills
○ lungs
○ a tail

2.3.1, 2.3.2

7 Which animal looks like its parents when it is born?

◯ a bear

◯ a butterfly

◯ a frog

2.3.1, 2.3.2

8 How is a butterfly larva DIFFERENT from an adult butterfly?

◯ The larva is not living.

◯ The larva does not need food to live.

◯ The larva does not look like the adult butterfly.

2.3.1, 2.3.2

9 Which stage of the butterfly life cycle does this picture show?

◯ adult

◯ larva

◯ pupa

2.3.1

10 Which is the correct order of stages in the metamorphosis of a frog?

◯ egg, frog, tadpole

◯ egg, tadpole, frog

◯ frog, tadpole, egg

2.3.1

11 At what stage of its life cycle does an animal reproduce?

○ when it is born

○ when it dies

○ when it is an adult

2.3.2

12 How is a tiger cub DIFFERENT from a tadpole?

○ A tiger cub does not hatch from an egg.

○ A tiger cub does not look like an adult tiger.

○ A tiger cub hatches from an egg.

2.3.1

13 You plant a bean seed in a cup of soil. Which plant part will grow from the seed FIRST?

○ flowers

○ leaves

○ roots

2.3.1, 2.3.2

14 Tina does an experiment with two plants. She gives Plant 1 fresh water. She gives Plant 2 salt water. The pictures show the results of Tina's experiment.

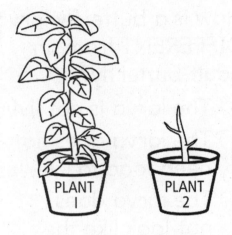

What can you infer?

○ These plants grow better with salt water than with fresh water.

○ These plants grow better with fresh water than with salt water.

○ These plants grow the same with either fresh water or salt water.

2.3.2

15 Which is TRUE?

○ Some plants live longer than others.

○ All animals go through metamorphosis.

○ Plants begin their life cycle as eggs.

2.3.1

16 Which is the correct order of the life cycle of a plant?

○ adult plant, seed, seedling

○ seedling, seed, adult plant

○ seed, seedling, adult plant

2.3.1, 2.3.2

17 Which part of the plant life cycle does this picture show?

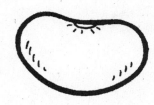

○ adult plant

○ seed

○ seedling

2.3.1

18 What happens at the BEGINNING of a plant's life cycle?

○ The plant dies.

○ The plant grows flowers.

○ The seed germinates.

2.3.2

19 How are a peach and a pinecone the SAME?

○ They grow on the same type of tree.

○ They both hold seeds.

○ They are both fruit.

2.3.2

20 Which starts its life cycle as a seed?

○ an apple tree

○ a butterfly

○ an elephant

Designs to Meet Needs

STANDARD 4
Science, Engineering and Technology

The Pyramids, Indianapolis, Indiana

I Wonder How

An engineer planned a design for these buildings. How? *Turn the page to find out.*

Here's How An engineer drew a plan for the buildings. The plan showed these interesting shapes.

Track Your Progress

Essential Questions and Indiana Standards

STANDARD 4
Science, Engineering and Technology

Describe how technologies have been developed to meet human needs.

2.4.1 Identify parts of the human body as tools, such as hands for grasping and teeth for cutting and chewing. **2.4.2** Identify technologies developed by humans to meet a human need and investigate the limitations of the technology and how it has improved quality of life.

Essential Question

How Are Body Parts Like Tools?

Engage Your Brain!

Find the answer to the question in the lesson.

How are your teeth like a knife?

Both can

_____

Active Reading

Lesson Vocabulary

❶ Preview the lesson.

❷ Write the 2 vocabulary terms here.

_____   _____

Tools of the Trade

A knife cuts. A broom sweeps. A knife and a broom are tools. A **tool** is something made to help people do work.

Parts of your body can work as tools. Teeth can cut. Arms can lift and throw. Hands can grasp. What else can your body parts do?

Active Reading

Find the sentence that tells the meaning of **tool**. Draw a line under the sentence.

Arms and hands pull the swimmer through water.

Oars pull a boat through water.

teeth

ax

Both the teeth and the ax cut and chop.

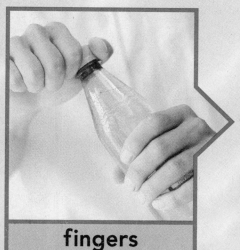

fingers

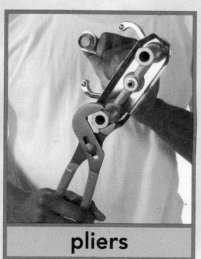

pliers

The fingers and the pliers twist and screw.

Do the Math!

Body Part Measurements

Find each measurement in inches. Then answer the questions.

your height _____

your arm span from fingertip to fingertip _____

your foot length _____

1. Which measurements are about the same?

_____

2. About how many foot lengths equal one arm span? _____

227

A Leg Up

If someone doesn't have a body part, engineers can sometimes help. Some engineers make artificial body parts. **Artificial** means made by humans. Artificial body parts can take the place of some real body parts.

Artificial body parts don't always look like real ones. But they help people who need them. With artificial body parts, these people can do the same things other people do.

Active Reading

An effect tells what happens. Draw two lines under an effect of using artificial body parts.

This boy uses an artificial leg to play sports.

© Houghton Mifflin Harcourt Publishing Company (©Richard T. Nowitz/Photo Researchers, Inc.

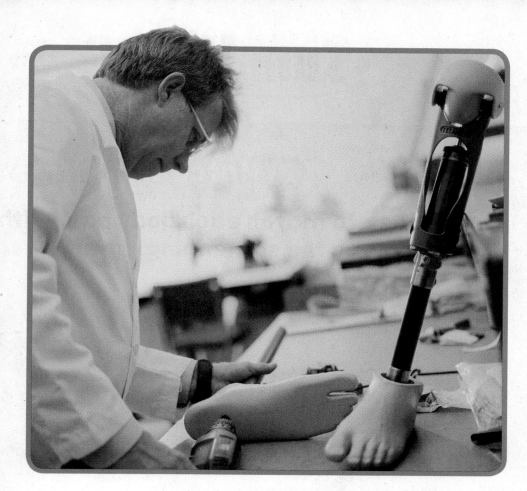

This engineer is working on an artificial leg and foot.

This artificial leg does not look like a real one. But it helps the man run nearly as well as he could with a real leg.

Sum It Up!

1 Match It!

Draw a line to match each body part with the tool that does the same thing.

2 Write It!

Write to tell how artificial body parts help people.

_____

_____

_____

Name _____

Word Play

Write a word from the box next to each body part to tell what it does.

lift	grasp	cut

_____

_____

_____

Apply Concepts

Complete the diagram. Tell how the real leg and the artificial leg are the same and different.

Real Leg	Artificial Leg
	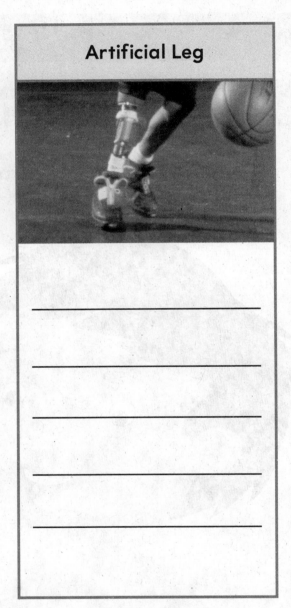
_____	_____
_____	_____
_____	_____
_____	_____
_____	_____

Take It Home!

Family Members: As you and your child do everyday activities, such as eating or walking, ask your child to demonstrate and explain how body parts act as tools.

Design Process As citizens of the constructed world, students will participate in the design process. Students will learn to use materials and tools safely and employ the basic principles of the engineering design process in order to find solutions to problems.

Essential Question

What Is the Design Process?

Engage Your Brain!

Find the answer to the question in the lesson.

How could you keep the dog leashes from getting tangled?

You could

_____

Active Reading

Lesson Vocabulary

1 Preview the lesson.

2 Write the 2 vocabulary terms here.

_____   _____

Get Real!

Look at the engineers at work! **Engineers** solve problems by using math and science. The answers they find help people in the real world.

Engineers work in many areas. Some engineers design cars. Some make robots. Others find ways to make the world cleaner or safer.

Active Reading

Find the sentence that tells the meaning of **engineers**. Draw a line under that sentence.

A civil engineer plans bridges and roads.

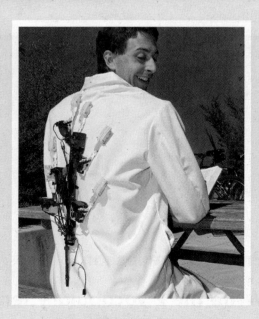

A robotics engineer designs robots.

The Design Process

How do engineers solve a problem? They use a design process. A **design process** is a set of steps that engineers follow to solve problems.

This engineer checks on a building project.

An aerospace engineer may work on airplanes or rockets.

▶ Circle the names of three kinds of engineers.

© Houghton Mifflin Harcourt Publishing Company (bkgd) ©Radius Images/Corbis; (b) ©James Blair/NASA/Handout/CNP/Corbis

A Tangled Mess!

When Kate walks her dogs, their leashes always get tangled. She needs to solve this problem. How can a design process help?

Active Reading

Why is there a number next to each heading?

1 Find a problem. Brainstorm ideas.

Kate's first step is to name her problem. What is wrong? What does Kate want to do? Kate brainstorms ways to solve her problem.

2 Keep good records.

Kate gets out her science notebook. She will keep good records. She will show how she plans and builds the solution to her problem.

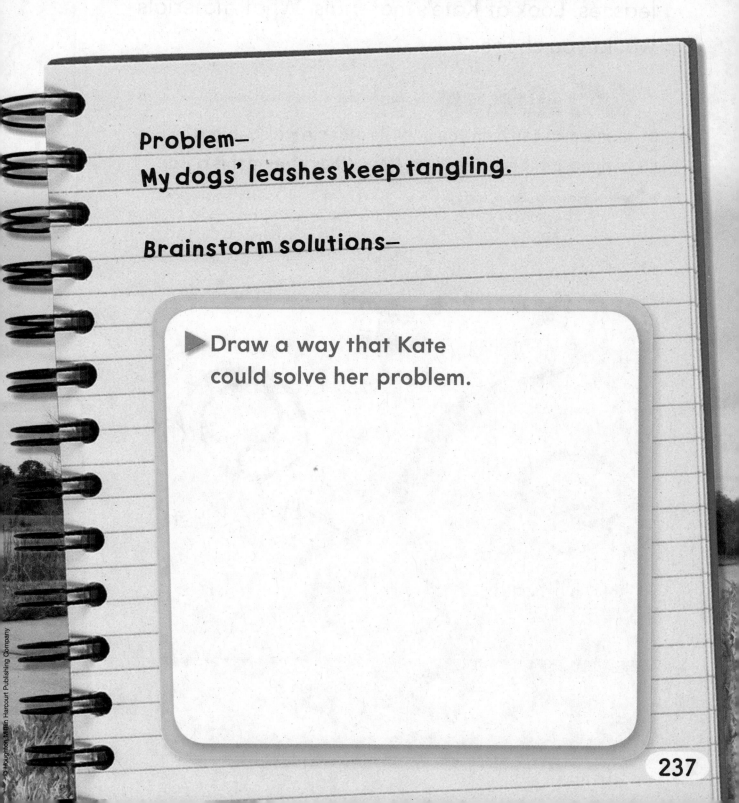

Problem—
My dogs' leashes keep tangling.

Brainstorm solutions—

▶ Draw a way that Kate could solve her problem.

3 Plan a solution. Choose materials.

Next, Kate chooses a solution to try. She makes a plan. She draws and labels her plan.

Kate chooses materials that are good for leashes. Look at Kate's materials. What materials would you choose?

Active Reading

Clue words can help you find the order in which things happen. **Next** is a clue word. Draw a box around this word.

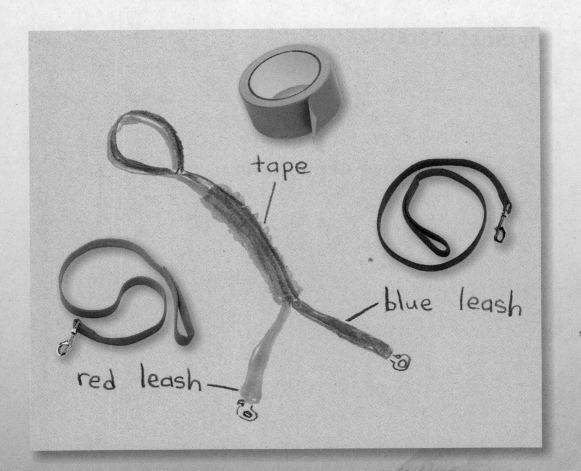

tape

blue leash

red leash

4 Build the solution.

Kate follows her plan to make her new leash.
The new leash may be the solution to her problem!

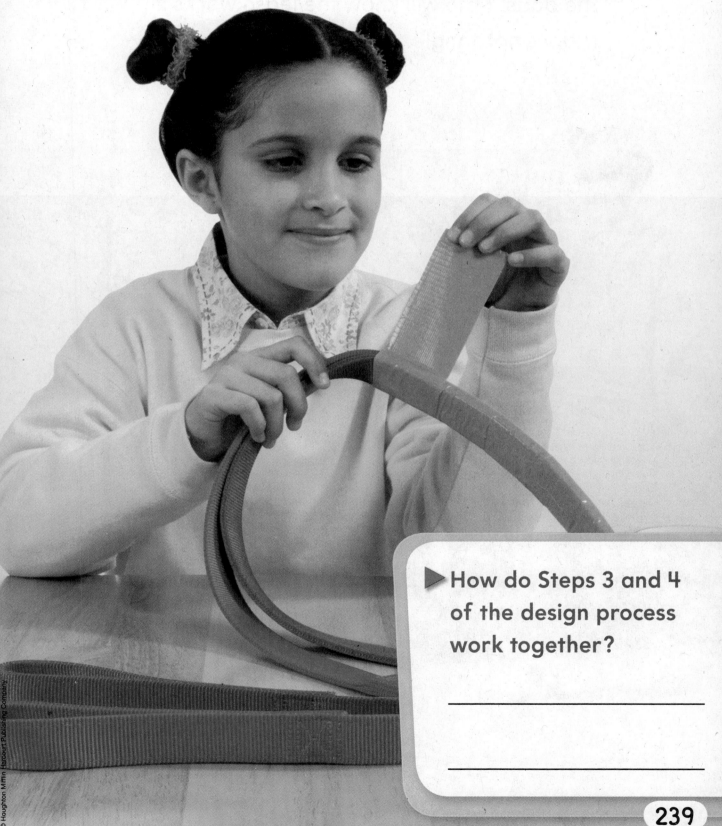

▶ How do Steps 3 and 4 of the design process work together?

_____

_____

5 Test the solution.

It is time for Kate to find out whether the new leash works. She tests it when she walks the dogs. Kate will know the leash works if it does not tangle.

6 Communicate the results.

Kate shows the results of her test. The design worked! Kate writes about what happened during the test. She takes a picture of her design. She also writes about how to make the next design better.

My Results—
1. Red and blue parts of the new leash did not tangle.
2. My feet bumped the dogs as I walked.

Ways to make the design better—make the leash parts or the handle longer.

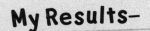

▶ Circle the part of the results that tells about a problem with the leash.

Sum It Up!

① Circle It!

Circle the step of the design process shown here.

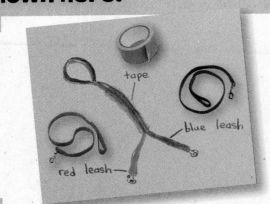

tape

blue leash

red leash

Test the solution.

Plan a solution.

Build the solution.

② Write It!

Write the answer to the question.

Why is it important to keep good records?

_____

_____

_____

_____

Name _____

Word Play

Write a term for each definition.

design process   materials   solution   test

Steps that engineers follow to solve a problem

__ __ __ __ __ __   __ __ __ __ __ __ __
   1   3 2

The answer to a problem

__ __ __ __ __ __ __ __
       4   5

How you find out whether a solution worked

__ __ __ __
  6

Things you use to make a design

__ __ __ __ __ __ __ __ __
    7 8

Solve the riddle. Write the numbered letters in order on the lines below.
I am a scientist who solves real-world problems. Who am I?

__ __ __ __ __ __ __ __
1 2 3 4 5 6 7 8

Apply Concepts

Complete the flowchart with the steps of the design process.

Design Process

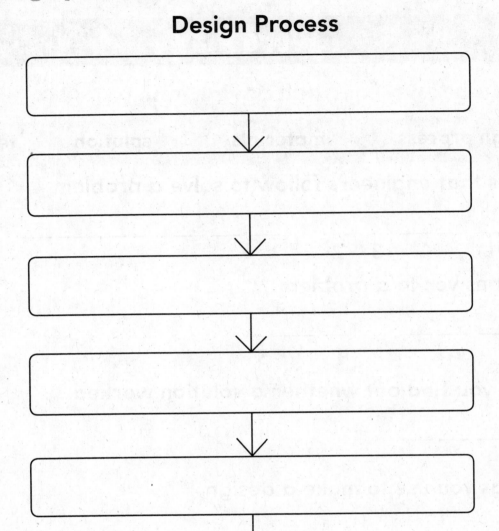

Inquiry Flipchart p. 29

2.4.3 Identify a need and design a simple tool to meet that need.

Lesson **3**
INQUIRY

Name _____

Essential Question

How Can We Use the Design Process?

Set a Purpose
Tell what you want to do.

_____

_____

Think About the Procedure

1 Why do you need to plan your solution?

_____

_____

_____

2 Why do you need to test your solution?

_____

_____

Record Your Data

Draw to communicate your solution and the test results. Label the materials. Write a caption to tell how your solution works.

_____

Draw Conclusions

How did the design process help you solve the problem?

_____

_____

Ask More Questions

What other questions could you ask about using the design process?

_____

_____

Ask a Roller Coaster Designer

What do roller coaster designers do?
We design roller coasters for amusement parks. We think up ideas for new rides. We also figure out how much they will cost to build.

Do designers work alone?
We work as a team with engineers to make a design. The design has to work and be safe and fun for riders. A factory then builds the ride.

How long does it take to build a roller coaster?
It usually takes about a year from design to finish. A simpler design takes less time.

Now It's Your Turn!

▶ What question would you ask a roller coaster designer?

_____

_____

_____

_____

Design Your Own Roller Coaster

▶ Draw your own roller coaster in the space below.

▶ Explain your design. Write about how your roller coaster moves.

_____

_____

_____

Name _____

Multiple Choice
Fill in the circle next to the best answer.

2.4.1

1 How can you use your arms as tools?

○ cross them across your chest

○ stretch them when you yawn

○ lift a heavy box

2.4.1

2 Which body part is this boy using as a tool when he kicks the ball?

○ his eye

○ his foot

○ his hand

2.4.1

3 Which body part can cut food like a knife?

○ an arm

○ an ear

○ teeth

2.4.1

4 How are fingers and pliers the SAME?

○ They are body parts.
○ They can grab things.
○ They are metal.

2.4.1

5 This boy is swimming. Which body parts is he using as tools?

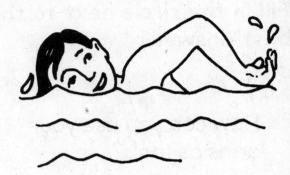

○ his arms and hands
○ his chest and stomach
○ his teeth and tongue

2.4.1

6 How can you use your hands as tools?

○ to grab things

○ to see things

○ to touch things

2.4.2

7 What does an artificial leg take the place of?

○ a missing real leg

○ a missing shoe

○ nothing

2.4.2

8 How is an artificial body part LIKE a real body part?

○ Both are covered with skin.

○ Both can help a person do things.

○ Both are made from metal.

2.4.2

9 Allie is missing one leg. Yesterday, she ran in a 5-mile race. How do you think Allie is able to run?

○ She uses a cane.

○ She runs with a friend.

○ She uses an artificial leg.

Design Process

10 What do engineers use to solve problems?

○ art and history

○ history and music

○ math and science

2.4.2

11 What kind of work do engineers do?

- ○ All engineers design robots.
- ○ All engineers design cars.
- ○ Different engineers do different kinds of work.

Design Process

12 Why do engineers use the design process?

- ○ It is easy.
- ○ It helps them solve problems.
- ○ It helps them use tools.

Use this information to answer questions 13–16.

Ethan has a problem. He wants to bring a water bottle with him when he rides his skateboard. He does not want to carry the bottle in his hand.

Design Process, 2.4.3

13 What process can Ethan use to help solve his problem?

- ○ the design process
- ○ the math process
- ○ the science process

Design Process, 2.4.3

14 Ethan has an idea for a solution. He wants to strap a bottle to his arm. What should he do next?

○ tell his friends about it

○ test his solution

○ plan a solution

Design Process, 2.4.3

15 How should Ethan plan his solution?

○ watch other children ride skateboards

○ draw and label the solution

○ test the solution

Design Process, 2.4.3

16 Ethan makes his bottle holder. Which step of the design process is Ethan doing?

○ Build the solution.

○ Plan a solution.

○ Communicate the results.

Design Process, 2.4.3

17 How can you tell whether a solution works?

○ ask other people

○ test the solution

○ draw and write about the solution

Design Process

18 What is the LAST step of the design process?

○ Choose materials.

○ Find a problem.

○ Communicate the results.

Design Process

19 You chose these items to design a solution to a problem. What step of the design process did you do?

- ◯ Test the solution.
- ◯ Plan a solution. Choose materials.
- ◯ Find a problem. Brainstorm ideas.

Design Process, 2.4.3

20 Rachel makes a shelf to hold all her books. She tests the shelf. Not all her books fit on the shelf. What should Rachel do with the results of this test?

- ◯ use them to design a better shelf that can fit all her books
- ◯ use them to help her choose the best materials for a shelf
- ◯ throw them away and find a new problem to solve

Interactive Glossary

This Interactive Glossary will help you learn how to spell and pronounce a vocabulary term. The Glossary will give you the meaning of the term. It will also show you a picture to help you understand what the term means.

Where you see **Your Turn** write your own words or draw your own picture to help you remember what the term means.

Glossary Pronunciation Key

With every glossary term, there is also a phonetic respelling. A phonetic respelling writes the word the way it sounds. This can help you pronounce new words. Use this key to help you understand the respellings.

Sound	As in	Phonetic Respelling	Sound	As in	Phonetic Respelling
a	bat	(BAT)	oo	pool	(POOL)
ah	lock	(LAHK)	ow	out	(OWT)
air	rare	(RAIR)	oy	foil	(FOYL)
ar	argue	(AR•gyoo)	s	cell	(SEL)
aw	law	(LAW)		sit	(SIT)
ay	face	(FAYS)	sh	sheep	(SHEEP)
ch	chapel	(CHAP•uhl)	th	that	(THAT)
e	test	(TEST)		thin	(THIN)
ee	eat	(EET)	u	pull	(PUL)
	feet	(FEET)	uh	medal	(MED•uhl)
	ski	(SKEE)		talent	(TAL•uhnt)
er	paper	(PAY•per)		pencil	(PEN•suhl)
	fern	(FERN)		onion	(UHN•yuhn)
eye	idea	(eye•DEE•uh)		playful	(PLAY•fuhl)
i	bit	(BIT)		dull	(DUHL)
ing	going	(GOH•ing)	y	yes	(YES)
k	card	(KARD)		ripe	(RYP)
	kite	(KYT)	z	bags	(BAGZ)
ngk	bank	(BANGK)	zh	treasure	(TREZH•er)
oh	over	(OH•ver)			

Interactive Glossary

A

artificial [ar·ti·FI·shuhl]
Made by humans. (p. 228)

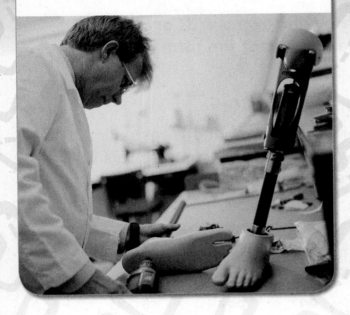

attract [uh·TRAKT]
To pull toward something.
(p. 123)

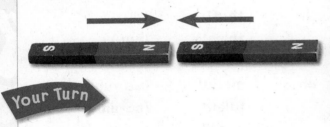

Your Turn

C

communicate
[kuh·MYOO·ni·kayt]
To write, draw, or speak to
show what you have learned.
(p. 29)

condensation
[kahn·duhn·SAY·shuhn]
The process by which water
vapor, a gas, changes into
liquid water. (p. 55)

D

condense [**kuhn**·DENS]

To change from a gas into tiny drops of water. (p. 155)

design process
[**dih**·ZYN PRAHS·**es**]

A set of steps that engineers follow to solve problems (p. 235)

Your Turn

cone [KOHN]

A part of a pine tree and some other plants where seeds form. (p. 212)

direction
[**di**·REK·**shuhn**]

The path that something is moving along. (p.103)

Your Turn

Interactive Glossary

dissolve [di·ZOLV]
To completely mix a solid with a liquid. (p. 66)

Your Turn

draw conclusions
[DRAW kuhn·KLOO·zhuhnz]
To use information gathered during an investigation to see whether the results support the hypothesis. (p. 29)

E

engineer [en·juh·NEER]
A person who uses math and science to design technology that solves problems. (p. 234)

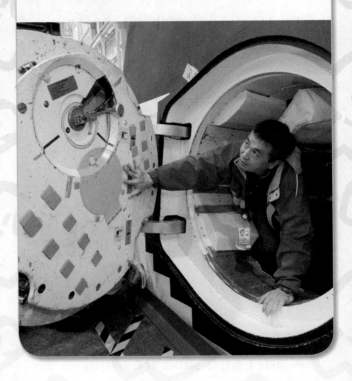

evaporate [ee·VAP·uh·rayt]
To change from a liquid into a gas. (p. 154)

evaporation
[ee·vap·uh·RAY·shuhn]
The process by which liquid water changes into water vapor, a gas. (p. 54)

F

force [FAWRS]
A push or a pull that makes an object move or stop moving. (p. 98)

Your Turn

G

gas [GAS]
A state of matter that fills all the space of its container. (p. 49)

germinate [JER·muh·nayt]
To start to grow. (p. 208)

Interactive Glossary

gravity [GRAV·ih·tee]
A force that pulls all things toward the center of Earth. (p. 114)

Your Turn

hurricane [HER·ih·kayn]
A large storm with heavy rain and strong winds. (p. 165)

hypothesis [hy·PAHTH·uh·sis]
A statement that you can test. (p. 27)

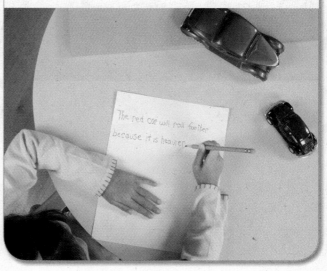

I

inquiry skills
[IN·**kwer·ee** SKILZ]

The skills people use to find out information. (p. 4)

investigate [in·VES·**tuh·gayt**]

To plan and do a test to answer a question or solve a problem. (p. 26)

L

larva
[LAHR·**vuh**]

Another name for a caterpillar. (p. 197)

Your Turn

life cycle [LYF SY·**kuhl**]

Changes that happen to an animal or a plant during its life. (p. 191)

Interactive Glossary

lightning [LYT·ning]
A flash of electricity in the sky. (p. 164)

liquid [LIK·wid]
A state of matter that takes the shape of its container. (p. 48)

M

magnet [MAG·nit]
An object that can pull things made of iron or steel and can push or pull other magnets. (p. 122)

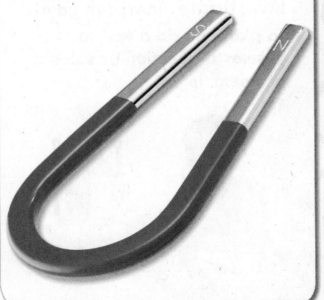

mass [MAS]

The amount of matter in an object. (p. 46)

matter [MAT·er]

Anything that takes up space and has mass. (p. 46)

Your Turn

metamorphosis [met·uh·MAWR·fuh·sis]

A series of changes that some animals go through. (p. 193)

mixture [MIKS·cher]

A mix of different kinds of matter. (p. 64)

Interactive Glossary

moon [MOON]

A large sphere, or ball of rock, in the sky that does not give off its own light. (p. 176)

Your Turn

motion [MOH·shuhn]

Movement. Things are in motion when they move. (p. 88)

P

phase [FAYZ]

One of several shapes the moon seems to have as it orbits Earth. (p. 177)

pole [POHL]

A place on a magnet where the pull is the greatest. (p. 122)

position
[puh·ZI·shuhn]

The location of an object in relation to a nearby object or place. (p. 102)

Your Turn

precipitation
[pri·sip·uh·TAY·shuhn]

Water that falls from the sky. Rain, snow, sleet, and hail are kinds of precipitation. (p. 144)

property [PRAH·per·tee]

One part of what something is like. Color, size, and shape are each a property. (p. 62)

Interactive Glossary

pull [PUL]

The tugging of an object closer to you. (p. 98)

push [PUSH]

The pressing of an object away from you. (p. 98)

R

pupa [PYOO·puh]

The part of a life cycle when a caterpillar changes into a butterfly. (p. 197)

repel [rih·PEL]

To push away from something. (p. 123)

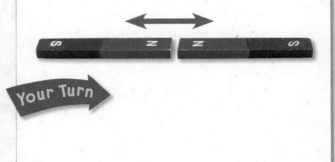

Your Turn

reproduce [ree·pruh·DOOS]

To have young, or more living things of the same kind. (p. 190)

season [SEE·zuhn]

A time of year that has a certain kind of weather. The four seasons are spring, summer, fall, and winter. (p. 156)

S

science tools [SY·uhns TOOLZ]

The tools people use to find out information. (p. 14)

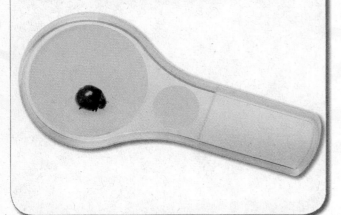

seed [SEED]

The part of a plant that new plants grow from. (p. 206)

Your Turn

Interactive Glossary

seedling [SEED·ling]
A young plant. (p. 209)

speed [SPEED]
The measure of how fast something moves. (p. 88)

solid [SAHL·id]
The only state of matter that has its own shape. (p. 47)

star [STAR]
An object in the sky that gives off its own light. The sun is the closest star to Earth. (p. 174)

T

sun [SUHN]
The star closest to Earth.
(p. 174)

tadpole [TAD·pohl]
A young frog that comes out of an egg and has gills to take in oxygen from the water. (p. 192)

Your Turn

temperature
[TEM·per·uh·cher]
A measure of how hot or cold something is. You can measure temperature with a thermometer.
(p. 144)

Interactive Glossary

thermometer
[ther·MAHM·uht·ter]
A tool used
to measure
temperature. (p. 15)

Your Turn

tool [TOOL]
Something used to make
work easier or something
used to do a particular job.
(p. 226)

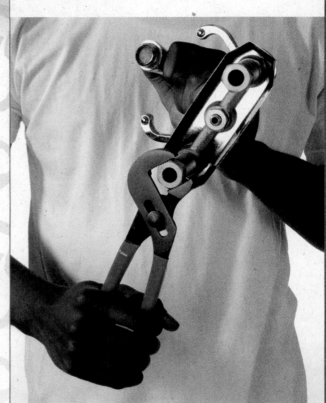

Your Turn

thunderstorm
[THUHN·der·stawrm]
A storm with a lot of rain,
thunder, and lightning. (p. 164)

tornado [tawr·NAY·doh]

A spinning cloud with a cone shape and very strong winds. (p. 165)

water cycle
[WAW·ter SY·kuhl]

The movement of water from Earth to the air and back again. (p. 154)

Your Turn

water vapor
[WAW·ter VAY·per]

Water in the form of a gas. (p. 50)

Interactive Glossary

weather [WEH·ther]
What the air outside is like.
(p. 140)

weather pattern
[WEH·ther PAT·ern] **A weather change that repeats over and over.** (p. 152)

wind [WIND]
Moving air that surrounds us and takes up space. (p. 144)

Your Turn

Index

Index

Index

Index